MASSACHUSETTS TEST PREP
PARCC Practice Book
English Language Arts
Grade 4

© 2015 by Test Master Press Massachusetts

All rights reserved. No part of this book may be reproduced or transmitted in any form or by any means, electronic, mechanical, photocopying, recording, or otherwise without prior written permission.

ISBN 978-1519591111

CONTENTS

Introduction — 4

Practice for the PARCC Assessments — 5

    Set 1: Literary Analysis Task — 6
    Set 2: Research Simulation Task — 22
    Set 3: Narrative Writing Task — 38
    Set 4: Short Informational Text — 46
    Set 5: Short Literary Text — 54
    Set 6: Long Informational Text — 62
    Set 7: Paired Literary Passages — 71

    Set 8: Literary Analysis Task — 79
    Set 9: Research Simulation Task — 95
    Set 10: Narrative Writing Task — 112
    Set 11: Short Informational Text — 121
    Set 12: Short Literary Text — 129
    Set 13: Long Informational Text — 136
    Set 14: Paired Informational Passages — 144

Answer Key — 153

    Set 1: Literary Analysis Task — 154
    Set 2: Research Simulation Task — 156
    Set 3: Narrative Writing Task — 158
    Set 4: Short Informational Text — 159
    Set 5: Short Literary Text — 160
    Set 6: Long Informational Text — 161
    Set 7: Paired Literary Passages — 162
    Set 8: Literary Analysis Task — 163
    Set 9: Research Simulation Task — 165
    Set 10: Narrative Writing Task — 167
    Set 11: Short Informational Text — 168
    Set 12: Short Literary Text — 169
    Set 13: Long Informational Text — 170
    Set 14: Paired Informational Passages — 171

INTRODUCTION
For Parents, Teachers, and Tutors

About the PARCC Assessments

The PARCC assessments are a set of tests that determine whether students have the skills and abilities listed in the Common Core State Standards. This practice book will prepare students for all the types of tasks found on the PARCC English Language Arts/Literacy tests.

About the Tasks on the PARCC Assessments

The PARCC assessments contain one of each of the following types of tasks.

Task	Details
Literary Analysis Task	Students read two literary passages and answer selected-response, technology-enhanced, and constructed-response questions. The final question is an essay question that assesses both reading and writing skills.
Research Simulation Task	Students read three informational passages and answer selected-response, technology-enhanced, and constructed-response questions. The final question is an essay question that requires students to synthesize information from both passages.
Narrative Task	Students read one literary passage and answer selected-response, technology-enhanced, and constructed-response questions. The final question requires students to write a narrative and assesses writing skills.
Short Literary or Informational Text	Students read one short passage and answer selected-response, technology-enhanced, and constructed-response questions.
*Long Literary or Informational Text	Students read one longer passage and answer selected-response, technology-enhanced, and constructed-response questions.
*Paired Literary or Informational Texts	Students read one set of paired passages. Students answer selected-response, technology-enhanced, and constructed-response questions about each passage. Students answer 1 or more questions that require using information from both passages.

*The PARCC assessment will include either a long passage or a set of paired passages. This practice book includes both types of tasks.

INTRODUCTION
For Parents, Teachers, and Tutors

Key Features of the PARCC Assessments

The PARCC assessments have key features that students will need to be familiar with. There are certain skills emphasized on the test, as well as question styles and formats that will be new to most students. These key features are described below.

- The PARCC tests have a greater emphasis on writing skills. Students will have to provide more written answers, as well as write essays and narratives.
- The PARCC tests include paired questions. A first question will ask about a text, and a second question will expand on the first, often by asking for evidence.
- The PARCC tests may be taken online and include technology-enhanced questions. These have a range of formats, and may involve tasks like placing items in order, highlighting sentences from a text, or completing webs and diagrams.
- The PARCC tests focus on close reading and using evidence from the texts. Questions will require students to read texts closely and to use specific evidence from the text.
- The PARCC tests involve more analysis and evaluation. Instead of only showing they comprehend texts, students will be asked questions that require them to analyze a text closely, evaluate a text, relate to a text, or form and support an opinion about a text.

PARCC Test Preparation

The practice sets in this book will prepare students for the tasks they need to complete on the real PARCC tests. There are sets for all the types of tasks found on the real tests. The questions within each set are similar to what students will find on the real PARCC tests, except that each set contains more questions than the real test. This will ensure that students experience all the types of questions they are likely to encounter on the real test.

This book has also been specifically designed to prepare students for the key features of the test. This includes having more written answer questions, paired questions, and questions that mimic the technology-enhanced questions. The skills assessed match the PARCC tests, with a greater focus on close reading, using evidence from text, and analyzing and evaluating texts.

About the Common Core State Standards

Student learning and assessment is based on the skills listed in the Massachusetts Curriculum Framework. This framework has the same content as the Common Core State Standards, except that a few additional skills are included. The PARCC tests and this book both cover all the skills listed in the Common Core State Standards.

PARCC Practice

Set 1

Literary Analysis Task

Instructions

This set has two passages for you to read. Read each passage and answer the questions that follow it.

For each multiple-choice question, fill in the circle for the correct answer. For other types of questions, follow the instructions given. Some of the questions require a written answer. Write your answer on the lines provided.

After reading both passages, you will answer an essay question. You will use information from both passages to answer this question. Write your answer on the lines provided.

The Girlfriend and the Mother

Prince Arnold had a very close bond with his mother. They shared everything with each other. They had remained close since he had been a child. One day, he met a girl named Chloe and she became his girlfriend. Gradually, Arnold began to spend more time with his girlfriend than with his mother.

Although he still enjoyed long conversations with his mother, she began to feel left out. She felt that the only time she would get to spend with him was in the evenings. This was when he would fall asleep on the couch and she would sit beside him and stroke his hair.

His mother really liked the gray strands that grew in his hair. She felt they made him look wise. So as she stroked his head she would remove some of the darker hairs from his scalp. She did this over many nights for an entire year.

Arnold's girlfriend had a similar habit. She thought that his gray hairs made him look old. So she would pluck as many gray hairs from his head as she possibly could. She too did this for many nights over the year.

After a year had gone by, Arnold found that he was almost completely bald. His mother and girlfriend had removed so much of his hair that he was left only with short little tufts. Both women and Arnold were unhappy with his new look. The ladies felt that their battle for his time had led to the problem.

"We're so sorry," they said. "What we have done is unfair."

They realized that they must all get along and spend time together if they were to remain happy. The mother and the girlfriend made a promise to be happy sharing Prince Arnold's time.

1. Read this sentence from the passage.

   His mother and girlfriend had removed so much of his hair that he was left only with short little tufts.

   What does the word <u>removed</u> mean?

   - Ⓐ Scared off
   - Ⓑ Fought over
   - Ⓒ Taken away
   - Ⓓ Changed places

2. Read this sentence from the passage.

   Prince Arnold had a very close bond with his mother.

   Which meaning of the word <u>bond</u> is used in the sentence?

   - Ⓐ To connect two or more items
   - Ⓑ A relationship or link between people
   - Ⓒ An agreement or promise
   - Ⓓ A type of glue

3 What is the mother's main problem in the passage?

- Ⓐ She dislikes her son's hair.
- Ⓑ She does not want to share her son.
- Ⓒ She argues with her son.
- Ⓓ She wants her son to get married.

4 "The Girlfriend and the Mother" is most like a –

- Ⓐ true story
- Ⓑ science fiction story
- Ⓒ biography
- Ⓓ fable

5 How are the girlfriend and the mother alike?

- Ⓐ They are both pleased when Arnold is bald.
- Ⓑ They both pluck out Arnold's hair.
- Ⓒ They both dislike Arnold's gray hair.
- Ⓓ They have both known Arnold since he was young.

6 How does the mother change in the passage?

- Ⓐ She realizes that her son is a grown man.
- Ⓑ She accepts her son's relationship with Chloe.
- Ⓒ She loses interest in her son.
- Ⓓ She learns that Chloe is a nice person.

7 Complete these sentences. Write **one** of the words below on each line.

royal   kind   old   unusual

wise   silly   young   special

Chloe thinks that Arnold's gray hair makes him look _____.

Arnold's mother thinks that his gray hair makes him look _____.

8 Based on your answer to Question 7, describe how their different feelings affect their actions.

_____

_____

_____

_____

_____

9. What will the mother most likely do next?

    Ⓐ   Come up with a plan to break up her son and Chloe

    Ⓑ   Start making an effort to spend time with her son and Chloe

    Ⓒ   Make her son think that his baldness is Chloe's fault

    Ⓓ   Start spending time with her husband instead of her son

10. How do you think Arnold feels at the end of the passage? Use details from the passage to explain why you think Arnold feels that way.

_____

_____

_____

_____

_____

_____

11 Use details from the passage to complete the cause and effect diagram below.

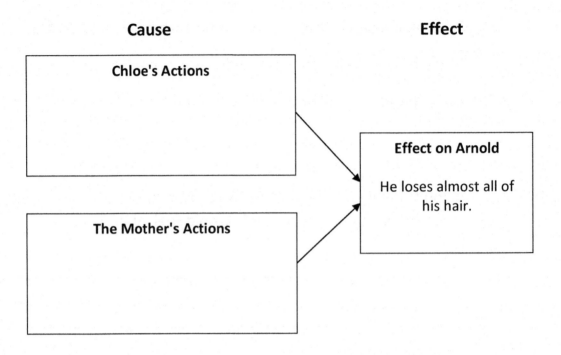

12 Describe what the art in the passage represents. Use details from the passage to support your answer.

_____

_____

_____

_____

_____

_____

One Game for Two

Thomas could be quite mean at times. He had a younger brother called Simon and he rarely shared his toys with him.

"You must share Thomas," urged his mother. "One day you will want somebody to share something with you and they won't. Then you will be very upset."

Thomas just laughed his mother's advice off.

"I'll be fine, Mom," he replied. "As long as I have my own toys, I will always be fine."

His mother just shrugged her shoulders.

"Very well," she said. "It seems that you know best."

One day she decided to teach him a lesson. Both boys had been begging for a video game system for over a year. She decided that it was finally time to buy the boys the video game system and a few games.

When Christmas day arrived, both boys were patiently waiting for their presents in front of the fireplace. As Thomas tore into the video game package, his eyes lit up. It was the exact video game system he had wanted for so long.

Simon took longer than Thomas to carefully unwrap his own present. When he did, he was delighted to see three video games. He thanked his mother for not just getting him one great game, but getting him three.

Thomas raced over to check out the games. He saw they were the games he wanted as well and grinned.

"There is just one thing, Simon," Simon's mother said. "You don't have a system to play them on, so you're going to have to ask if you can use your brother's."

Thomas's smile turned quickly into a frown.

"But it's my present," Thomas said gruffly. "I don't want him to use it."

"I think you should be kinder and let your brother use it," his mother suggested.

"Do I have to?" Thomas whined.

"You don't have to," his mother said. "But it would be the right thing to do."

Thomas just shrugged. Then he shook his head.

"No," he said firmly. "I've wanted it for ages and I don't want him to break it."

Simon looked at his brother sadly. He wasn't surprised by his decision, but he was still upset by it.

"Very well," the mother said. "But I hope you realize you won't have much fun with your video game system without any games to play."

Thomas suddenly realized that Simon had games, but he didn't. Simon started to say that Thomas could play his games, but his mother stopped him.

"Since you don't want to share your system with Simon, it wouldn't be fair for you to play his games," the mother continued.

Now Thomas realized that he had a problem. He had the system, Simon had the games, and they needed both to be able to play.

Thomas paused and thought for a moment.

"Okay, I suppose I could share my video game system," he whispered quietly. "That does seem fair."

Simon quickly agreed to share his games and they spent the rest of the day playing a racing game together.

13 Read this sentence from the passage.

> **He had a younger brother called Simon and he rarely shared his toys with him.**

Which word means the opposite of rarely?

- Ⓐ   Sometimes
- Ⓑ   Never
- Ⓒ   Often
- Ⓓ   Once

14 Read this sentence from the passage.

> **As Thomas tore into the video game package, his eyes lit up.**

The word tore suggests that Simon opened the package –

- Ⓐ   slowly
- Ⓑ   roughly
- Ⓒ   carefully
- Ⓓ   calmly

15 According to the passage, how is Simon different from Thomas?

  Ⓐ He is selfish.

  Ⓑ He is older.

  Ⓒ He is kinder.

  Ⓓ He is wiser.

16 Based on your answer to Question 15, describe **two** details that show what Simon is like.

  1: _____

  _____

  2: _____

  _____

17 Why does Thomas most likely grin when he sees the video games?

  Ⓐ He knows that Simon wanted them.

  Ⓑ He doesn't want to show that he is upset.

  Ⓒ He thinks that he will be able to play them.

  Ⓓ He expects his present to be the same.

18 The main theme of the passage is about –

- Ⓐ getting along with your siblings
- Ⓑ sharing your things with others
- Ⓒ buying good presents
- Ⓓ thinking of clever plans

19 Which sentence best supports your answer to Question 18?

- Ⓐ *One day you will want somebody to share something with you and they won't.*
- Ⓑ *One day she decided to teach him a lesson.*
- Ⓒ *Both boys had been begging for a video game system for over a year.*
- Ⓓ *I've wanted it for ages and I don't want him to break it.*

20 Circle the word below that best describes Thomas's mother. Explain why you made that choice.

        mean   **clever**

_____

_____

_____

_____

21 Why does Thomas finally decide to share his present with Simon? In what way is his decision still selfish? Use details from the passage to explain your answer.

_____

_____

_____

_____

_____

22 Read this sentence from the passage.

As Thomas tore into the video game package, his eyes lit up.

Explain what the phrase "his eyes lit up" shows about Thomas.

_____

_____

_____

_____

23 Read this section of the passage.

> Thomas's smile turned quickly into a frown.
>
> "But it's my present," Thomas said gruffly. "I don't want him to use it."
>
> "I think you should be kinder and let your brother use it," his mother suggested.
>
> "Do I have to?" Thomas whined.
>
> "You don't have to," his mother said. "But it would be the right thing to do."
>
> Thomas just shrugged. Then he shook his head.
>
> "No," he said firmly. "I've wanted it for ages and I don't want him to break it."

Circle **three** words that show that Thomas is grumpy. On the lines below, explain why you chose those words.

_____

_____

_____

_____

_____

_____

24 You have read two passages where characters learn to be less selfish. Write an essay describing what the mother in the first passage and Thomas in the second passage learn about being selfish.

- Explain what each character does that is selfish.
- Describe the problem that occurs because the character is selfish.
- Explain why each character becomes less selfish.
- Use details from both passages to support your answer.

END OF SET 1

PARCC Practice

Set 2

Research Simulation Task

Instructions

This set has three passages for you to read. Read each passage and answer the questions that follow it.

For each multiple-choice question, fill in the circle for the correct answer. For other types of questions, follow the instructions given. Some of the questions require a written answer. Write your answer on the lines provided.

After reading the three passages, you will answer an essay question. You will use information from all three passages to answer this question. Write your answer on the lines provided.

Muhammad Ali

Muhammad Ali is a famous American boxer. He was born in 1942. Many people believe that he is the greatest boxer of all time. Ali won the World Heavyweight Championship three times. He fought on four different continents. He had his first success as an amateur boxer. In 1960, he won an Olympic gold medal. During this time, he was known as Cassius Clay. He changed his name in 1964.

Ali became known as a fast and powerful fighter. He was also very confident. He often predicted which round he would win each fight. Some people thought he should be more humble, while others loved his attitude. He won his first title in 1964 after beating the fearsome Sonny Liston. Ali defended his title several times. By 1967, he was considered to be unbeatable. Then the Vietnam War occurred. Ali was meant to go to war, but he refused. He was unfairly stripped of his title. He was arrested and had his boxing license taken away. He fought the charges. He won his right to freedom. He also won the right to box again. In 1971, he continued his career.

He had lost some of his speed and power. However, he still reclaimed his title twice. He had famous bouts with Joe Frazier and George Foreman. He won both of these fights. His last fight was against Trevor Berbick in 1981. He was not as quick as usual, and he lost the fight.

He retired with a career record of 56 wins and 5 defeats. Ali now spends much of his time working with charities. In 1996, the Olympics were held in Atlanta. Ali was chosen to light the torch. It was a great way to honor a great sportsman.

His honors have not only been given to him for his sporting achievements. In 1999, he was awarded the Presidential Medal of Freedom. This is the highest medal an American civilian can receive. He was awarded the medal not only because of his sporting successes, but for his service to others and his efforts in promoting peace and equality. When awarding him the medal, President George W. Bush described Ali as "a fierce fighter and a man of peace." This is a good way to sum up Ali's achievements.

1   Read this sentence from the passage.

Ali became known as a fast and powerful fighter.

Which word means about the same as <u>powerful</u>?

- Ⓐ   Angry
- Ⓑ   Quick
- Ⓒ   Skilled
- Ⓓ   Strong

2   Choose the word that completes the definition of the word <u>reclaimed</u>. Write the word on the blank line.

after   more   less   again   before

claimed _____

3   Who did Ali defeat to win his first boxing title?

- Ⓐ   Sonny Liston
- Ⓑ   Joe Frazier
- Ⓒ   George Foreman
- Ⓓ   Trevor Berbick

4 The passage is most like –

    Ⓐ   a biography

    Ⓑ   an advertisement

    Ⓒ   an autobiography

    Ⓓ   a news article

5 Which detail from the passage is least important to the main idea?

    Ⓐ   Ali is thought of as the greatest boxer of all time.

    Ⓑ   Ali fought on four different continents.

    Ⓒ   Ali won his first world title in 1964.

    Ⓓ   Ali had 56 wins and 5 defeats.

6 Select **all** the sentences below that contain opinions.

    ☐   *In 1960, he won an Olympic gold medal.*

    ☐   *During this time, he was known as Cassius Clay.*

    ☐   *He was unfairly stripped of his title.*

    ☐   *Some people thought he should be more humble, while others loved his attitude.*

    ☐   *His last fight was against Trevor Berbick in 1981.*

    ☐   *It was a great way to honor a great sportsman.*

7 Which sentence from the passage best supports the idea that Ali was a successful boxer?

- Ⓐ *Ali won the World Heavyweight Championship three times.*
- Ⓑ *During this time, he was known as Cassius Clay.*
- Ⓒ *He often predicted which round he would win each fight.*
- Ⓓ *Ali now spends much of his time working with charities.*

8 How is the passage mainly organized?

- Ⓐ A problem is described and then a solution is given.
- Ⓑ Events are described in the order they occurred.
- Ⓒ Facts are given to support an argument.
- Ⓓ A question is asked and then answered.

9 Complete the web below by listing **three** actions that were taken against Ali when he refused to take part in the Vietnam War.

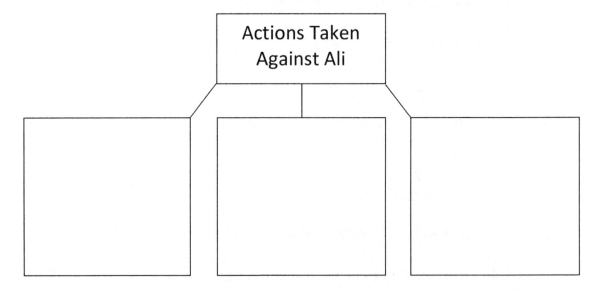

Abraham Lincoln

Abraham Lincoln was the 16th President of the United States. He was born in 1809. He died on April 15, 1865. Lincoln served the United States as President for just short of five years. He is remembered for his strong leadership skills. He led the nation through several conflicts, including the American Civil War.

Abraham Lincoln was born into a poor family. He was mostly self-educated. He worked as a country lawyer. During this period of his life, he also started a family. He raised four children.

His career in politics began at the state level. He was fiercely against slavery. He fought it through national debates. He gave public speeches about the issue. He wrote letters to persuade others to agree with him. His strong opinion won him the support of many. He was then elected president in 1860.

In April 1861, the American Civil War began. Lincoln planned to defeat the South. He wanted to reunify the nation. He oversaw the war effort very closely. He skillfully prevented British support for the South in late 1861. He took control of the civil conflict during the next two years. In 1863, he issued an order that ended slavery. Over 3 million slaves were freed. The war came to an end in 1865. Lincoln achieved his goal of uniting the nation.

Abraham Lincoln was shot and killed just six days after the end of the war. It was a sad end for a man who achieved so much. Abraham Lincoln is thought of by many as the greatest president of all time.

10 Read this sentence from the passage.

He was fiercely against slavery.

As it is used in the sentence, what does the word <u>fiercely</u> mean?

Ⓐ   Usually

Ⓑ   Quickly

Ⓒ   Strongly

Ⓓ   Strangely

11 Read this sentence from the passage.

He wanted to reunify the nation.

If the word <u>unify</u> means "to bring together," what does the word <u>reunify</u> mean?

Ⓐ   To bring together more

Ⓑ   To bring back together

Ⓒ   To stop bringing together

Ⓓ   To bring together before

12 In which year did Abraham Lincoln become president? Circle the correct answer.

1860   1861   1862   1863   1864   1865

13 Which paragraph has the main purpose of describing Abraham Lincoln's achievements during the war?

Ⓐ   Paragraph 1

Ⓑ   Paragraph 2

Ⓒ   Paragraph 4

Ⓓ   Paragraph 5

14 In which sentence from the passage does the author give a personal opinion about Lincoln?

Ⓐ   *Abraham Lincoln was the 16th President of the United States.*

Ⓑ   *In 1863, he issued an order that ended slavery.*

Ⓒ   *Abraham Lincoln was shot and killed just six days after the end of the war.*

Ⓓ   *It was a sad end for a man who achieved so much.*

15   Which detail about Abraham Lincoln is least important to understanding why he is considered by some as the greatest president of all time?

   Ⓐ   He achieved his goal of unifying the nation.

   Ⓑ   He fought to end slavery.

   Ⓒ   He was born into a poor family.

   Ⓓ   He led America through the Civil War.

16   Complete the web below using information from the passage.

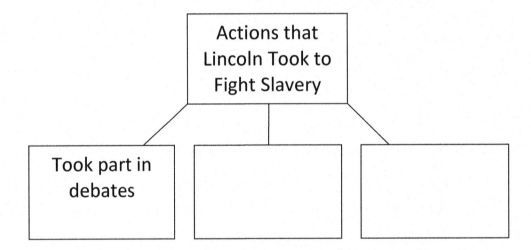

17 The passage describes Abraham Lincoln's achievements. Describe **two** of Lincoln's achievements.

1: _____

_____

2: _____

_____

18 The passage describes how Lincoln was born into a poor family and was mostly self-educated. Describe how these details affect how you feel about his achievements.

_____

_____

_____

_____

_____

_____

_____

_____

Amelia Earhart

Born in 1897, Amelia Earhart is an American aviation pioneer. She was the first woman to fly solo across the Atlantic Ocean. At that time, it was rare for females to be pilots, let alone be record-breaking pilots! In fact, Earhart was only the 16th woman to be given a pilot's license. She had to fight to achieve her dream of becoming a pilot, and was always having to prove herself to those who thought that women could not handle flying. Earhart set many other aviation records during her life, and also wrote about her experiences. She became a celebrity in the United States, and appeared in many advertisements.

The Purdue University funded an ill-fated flight of the globe in 1937. Sadly, Amelia Earhart and her navigator disappeared over the central Pacific Ocean. To this day, it is unknown what actually happened. Some researchers believe that the plane crashed into the ocean and sank. Another theory is that Amelia landed at an uninhabited island called Gardner Island. There have been many other theories, but none have yet to be proven. It may never be known what happened to Amelia Earhart. However, she can still always be remembered as a great pilot who achieved many incredible things.

19   What does the word ill-fated suggest about the flight funded by Purdue University?

   Ⓐ   It cost too much.

   Ⓑ   It ended badly.

   Ⓒ   It was poorly planned.

   Ⓓ   It did not take place.

20   Amelia Earhart was the first woman to fly solo across which ocean?

   Ⓐ   Atlantic Ocean

   Ⓑ   Pacific Ocean

   Ⓒ   Arctic Ocean

   Ⓓ   Indian Ocean

21   Which sentence best supports the idea that Earhart gained recognition for her achievements?

   Ⓐ   *In fact, Earhart was only the 16th woman to be given a pilot's license.*

   Ⓑ   *She became a celebrity in the United States, and appeared in many advertisements.*

   Ⓒ   *Sadly, Amelia Earhart and her navigator disappeared over the central Pacific Ocean.*

   Ⓓ   *It may never be known what happened to Amelia Earhart.*

22 Why was Amelia Earhart a pioneer? Use details from the passage in your answer.

_____

_____

_____

_____

_____

23 What is the main purpose of the second paragraph? Use details from the passage to support your answer.

_____

_____

_____

_____

_____

24 Do you think Amelia Earhart's solo flight would be as significant if it occurred today? Explain why or why not.

25 The passages all describe a person who achieved great things. To achieve great things, you often have to overcome challenges. Write an essay that describes how you have to overcome challenges to achieve great things.

- In your essay, describe how Ali, Lincoln, and Earhart achieved great things.
- Tell how they all had to overcome challenges to achieve great things.

END OF SET 2

PARCC Practice

Set 3

Narrative Writing Task

Instructions

This set has one passage for you to read. The passage is followed by questions.

Read each question carefully. For each multiple-choice question, fill in the circle for the correct answer. For other types of questions, follow the instructions given. Some of the questions require a written answer. Write your answer on the lines provided.

The last question requires you to write a story. Write your answer on the lines provided.

The Change

Maria was a beautiful young girl. She had long flowing blond hair and stunning blue eyes. Maria was still very insecure about her appearance. She often thought that most of her friends were prettier than her. One day a new girl joined her school. Her name was Sarah. Sarah had wavy dark brown hair and emerald green eyes. Maria wished she looked like her new friend. Over time she became jealous of Sarah.

One day, Maria decided to take action. She thought that if she looked like Sarah then she would feel much better. So she took her allowance money and headed to the mall with her older sister Bronwyn. She visited a hair salon and purchased some colored hair dye. When she returned home, she told her mother what she planned to do.

"It's your decision," said her mother sadly. "But I think you look beautiful as you are."

Maria ignored her mother's words and headed to the bathroom. She spent several hours dying her hair dark brown. She felt much better and skipped her way into school the following day. As she reached her class she noticed a new blond girl sitting near the front. She realized that it was Sarah. Her friend had dyed her hair a lighter shade of blond. It was almost identical to how Maria's had looked before. Sarah turned around and Maria spoke to her.

"Why did you dye your hair?" Maria asked.

"Well, I always loved your gorgeous blond hair," Sarah replied. "I thought it would be cool if we matched."

Maria slumped in her chair and sighed.

1   Read this sentence from the passage.

> **Maria was still very insecure about her appearance.**

If the word <u>secure</u> means "confident," what does the word <u>insecure</u> mean?

- Ⓐ   More confident
- Ⓑ   Less confident
- Ⓒ   Not confident
- Ⓓ   Most confident

2   Read this sentence from the passage.

> **Sarah had wavy dark brown hair and emerald green eyes.**

Which word means the opposite of <u>dark</u>?

- Ⓐ   Short
- Ⓑ   Light
- Ⓒ   Deep
- Ⓓ   Bright

3   Who is the main character in the passage? Circle the correct answer.

Sarah   Maria   Maria's mother

4 Think about your answer to Question 3. Describe **two** features of the passage that help show who the main character is.

Feature 1:

_____

_____

Feature 2:

_____

_____

5 Read this sentence from the passage.

> **She felt much better and skipped her way into school the following day.**

What does the word <u>skipped</u> suggest about Maria?

- Ⓐ She felt nervous.
- Ⓑ She was happy.
- Ⓒ She moved quietly.
- Ⓓ She was running late.

6 How would the passage be different if it was told from Maria's point of view?

Ⓐ   The reader would dislike Sarah more.

Ⓑ   The reader would learn how to dye hair.

Ⓒ   The reader would understand her feelings more.

Ⓓ   The reader would want to be like Maria.

7 What is Maria's main problem in the passage?

Ⓐ   She does not feel good about her looks.

Ⓑ   She does not have enough friends.

Ⓒ   She has never dyed her hair before.

Ⓓ   She wants Sarah to like her.

8 Read the list of Maria's actions in the story. Order the actions from first to last by writing the numbers 1, 2, 3, and 4 on the lines.

___   She tells her mother she is going to dye her hair.

___   She goes to the mall with her sister.

___   She learns that Sarah has dyed her hair.

___   She goes to the bathroom to dye her hair.

9   What is the main message of the passage?

    Ⓐ   Talk about your problems.

    Ⓑ   Be willing to change.

    Ⓒ   Listen to the people around you.

    Ⓓ   Be happy with yourself.

10 Based on your answer to Question 9, which sentence spoken by a character summarizes the main idea?

    Ⓐ   *"It's your decision."*

    Ⓑ   *"But I think you look beautiful as you are."*

    Ⓒ   *"Why did you dye your hair?"*

    Ⓓ   *"I thought it would be cool if we matched."*

11 At the end of the story, the author describes how Maria "slumped in her chair and sighed." How do you think Maria feels at this point? In your answer, explain why she feels that way.

    _____

    _____

    _____

    _____

12 The passage tells about a girl who is jealous of how someone else looks. Think of another reason someone might be jealous of someone else. Write a story about a character who is jealous of someone else. In your story, tell how the character learns not to be jealous.

_____

_____

_____

_____

_____

_____

_____

_____

_____

_____

_____

_____

_____

_____

END OF SET 3

PARCC Practice

Set 4

Short Informational Text

Instructions

This set has one passage for you to read. The passage is followed by questions.

Read each question carefully. For each multiple-choice question, fill in the circle for the correct answer. For other types of questions, follow the instructions given. Some of the questions require a written answer. Write your answer on the lines provided.

Robert De Niro

Robert De Niro is an American actor. He is known as one of the finest actors of his time. He has starred in a number of blockbuster films. He has also won many awards.

He was born in 1943 in New York City. De Niro left high school at the age of sixteen. He wanted to have a career in acting. He dreamed of appearing in Hollywood films. He studied acting between 1959 and 1963. He then took part in several small films.

His first major film role arrived in 1973. It was in the film *Bang the Drum Slowly*. After this, he won a role in the film *The Godfather Part II*. The film is one of the greatest films in history. He won the Academy Award for Best Supporting Actor for this role. It was the start of a great career. He was then given the lead role in many films.

During this time, he became good friends with Martin Scorsese. Scorsese was a successful director. They began to work together often. Their first film together was *Mean Streets* in 1973. De Niro won the Academy Award for Best Actor for this role. In 1980, he starred in the film *Raging Bull*. Scorsese was the director again. And again, De Niro won an Academy Award. They have worked on a number of box office hits over the years including *Casino*, *Cape Fear*, and *The Departed*.

His career continued. Over three decades, he has starred in many films. These have even included comedies like *Meet the Parents* and *Analyze This*.

In 2011, he was awarded a Golden Globe called the Cecil B. DeMille Award. This award is given for "outstanding contributions to the world of entertainment." Winners of the award in other years have included some great actors and directors including Steven Spielberg, Harrison Ford, Morgan Freeman, and Jodie Foster. It is also another achievement he shared with Martin Scorsese. Scorsese received the award in 2010.

Robert De Niro Films

Year	Title
1973	*Bang the Drum Slowly*
1974	*The Godfather Part II*
1976	*Taxi Driver*
1977	*New York, New York*
1980	*Raging Bull*
1986	*The Mission*
1987	*The Untouchables*
1988	*Midnight Run*
1990	*Goodfellas*
1991	*Backdraft*
1991	*Cape Fear*
1993	*A Bronx Tale*
1995	*Casino*
1995	*Heat*
1998	*Ronin*
1999	*Analyze This*
2000	*Meet the Parents*
2002	*Showtime*
2006	*The Good Shepherd*
2006	*The Departed*
2009	*Everybody's Fine*
2011	*Limitless*
2012	*Silver Linings Playbook*
2013	*Last Vegas*

Fun Fact

There is one other surprising link between De Niro and Scorsese. They were both the voices of characters in the 2004 animated comedy film *Shark Tale*. De Niro is the voice of a shark and Scorsese is the voice of a pufferfish!

1. As it is used in paragraph 1, what does <u>finest</u> mean?

    Ⓐ   Best

    Ⓑ   Smallest

    Ⓒ   Rarest

    Ⓓ   Nicest

2. Which of these does the table best show?

    Ⓐ   How many awards De Niro has won

    Ⓑ   How many times De Niro worked with Scorsese

    Ⓒ   How long De Niro has been acting for

    Ⓓ   How De Niro chooses his roles

3. Describe **two** more things the table shows about De Niro and his career.

    1: _____

    _____

    2: _____

    _____

4 Determine whether each sentence in paragraph 3 is a fact or an opinion. Write F or O on each line to show your choice.

___ His first major film role arrived in 1973.

___ It was in the film *Bang the Drum Slowly*.

___ After this, he won a role in the film *The Godfather Part II*.

___ The film is one of the greatest films in history.

___ He won the Academy Award for Best Supporting Actor for this role.

___ It was the start of a great career.

___ He was then given the lead role in many films.

5 How is the passage mainly organized?

Ⓐ A solution to a problem is described.

Ⓑ A question is asked and then answered.

Ⓒ A series of events are described in order.

Ⓓ Two different actors are compared.

6 The passage was probably written mainly to –

Ⓐ encourage people to become actors

Ⓑ describe the life of Robert De Niro

Ⓒ tell a funny story about a movie star

Ⓓ teach readers how to break into films

7 According to the passage, how are Robert De Niro and Martin Scorsese similar?

- Ⓐ They were both born in New York.
- Ⓑ They are both good actors.
- Ⓒ They both direct movies.
- Ⓓ They are both successful.

8 Based on your answer to Question 7, describe **two** details given in the passage that support your answer.

1: _____

_____

2: _____

_____

9 How would this passage be different if it were an autobiography?

- Ⓐ It would be a more factual summary of De Niro's life.
- Ⓑ It would include references to prove the statements made.
- Ⓒ It would include quotes from other sources.
- Ⓓ It would be De Niro's account of his own life.

10 Give **two** details the author includes to support the idea that De Niro and Scorsese are a good team.

Supporting Detail 1:

_____

_____

Supporting Detail 2:

_____

_____

11 Read this sentence about winners of the Cecil B. DeMille Award.

> **Winners of the award in other years have included some great actors and directors including Steven Spielberg, Harrison Ford, Morgan Freeman, and Jodie Foster.**

What does this sentence help you understand about the significance of De Niro receiving the award?

_____

_____

_____

_____

_____

12 How does the author show that Robert De Niro is a successful actor? Use at least **three** details from the passage to support your answer.

END OF SET 4

PARCC Practice

Set 5

Short Literary Text

Instructions

This set has one passage for you to read. The passage is followed by questions.

Read each question carefully. For each multiple-choice question, fill in the circle for the correct answer. For other types of questions, follow the instructions given. Some of the questions require a written answer. Write your answer on the lines provided.

Catching Up

June 15, 2013

Dear Sally,

I am writing to see how you are doing at college. Are you settling in well? I remember how upset you got when we dropped you off. I hate to think of you as being unhappy. I know what a bright and cheerful girl you are. It is hard to imagine you any other way! I am sure that you have already made a lot of new friends. How are your courses going? Are you enjoying the work and learning a lot? I bet you are finding it very interesting. I am so proud of you for studying and working your way toward your goals. It is motivating me in my own studies.

Everything is fine at home. I am halfway through my exams and have been enjoying them so far. I am prepared and relaxed when I attend each one. So far, they have all been a piece of cake. If all goes well, I may even be following in your footsteps in a few years time. We could even find ourselves at the same college. Having said that, I am not sure how much work we would actually get done! Knowing us we would either be having too much fun or wasting time with silly arguments. Seriously though, I really miss our chats.

Dad and Mom are great as always. Dad is working hard at his new job. It is going very well, and he may even have to travel to London soon. Mom is trying to get fit for our summer vacation. I know you can't make it, but you will be sorely missed. I am hoping that you will be able to make it back next year to travel with us. Any trip abroad is just not the same without you! I do understand, though. I know you are working hard and that it is all for your future.

Please write back to me when you get the chance. Until then, you will remain in my thoughts.

Lots of love,

Rory

1   Read this sentence from the passage.

I am prepared and relaxed when I attend each one.

Which word could best be used in place of <u>prepared</u>?

- Ⓐ   Calm
- Ⓑ   Ready
- Ⓒ   Studied
- Ⓓ   Patient

2   As it is used in the sentence below, what does <u>sorely</u> mean?

I know you can't make it, but you will be sorely missed.

- Ⓐ   Certainly
- Ⓑ   Suddenly
- Ⓒ   Sadly
- Ⓓ   Greatly

3   What is the second paragraph mostly about?
- Ⓐ   What Rory has been doing at home
- Ⓑ   What Rory imagines his sister is doing
- Ⓒ   Why Rory misses his sister
- Ⓓ   What Rory plans to do after school

4 Read this sentence from the passage.

So far, they have all been a piece of cake.

The phrase "a piece of cake" means that something is –

Ⓐ easy

Ⓑ tasty

Ⓒ quick

Ⓓ funny

5 The reader can conclude that Sally is Rory's –

Ⓐ older sister

Ⓑ younger sister

Ⓒ twin sister

Ⓓ mother

6 Think about how Rory feels about his sister not being able to go on the family vacation. Write the **two** words that best describe how he feels on the lines below.

pleased   excited   angry   surprised

upset   shocked   understanding   confused

Rory feels _____ but _____.

7 Based on your answer to Question 6, choose **three** sentences from the third paragraph that support your answer. Circle the **three** sentences below. Then explain what each sentence you chose shows about how he feels.

> Dad and Mom are great as always. Dad is working hard at his new job. It is going very well, and he may even have to travel to London soon. Mom is trying to get fit for our summer vacation. I know you can't make it, but you will be sorely missed. I am hoping that you will be able to make it back next year to travel with us. Any trip abroad is just not the same without you! I do understand, though. I know you are working hard and that it is all for your future.

1: _____

_____

2: _____

_____

3: _____

_____

8 Rory would be most likely to say that he is –

Ⓐ embarrassed by Sally

Ⓑ proud of Sally

Ⓒ jealous of Sally

Ⓓ confused by Sally

9 Based on the passage, what can you conclude about Rory and Sally?

Ⓐ They are very close.

Ⓑ They want similar careers.

Ⓒ They are the same age.

Ⓓ They have similar hobbies.

10 Do you think that Rory admires his sister? Use details from the passage to support your answer.

_____

_____

_____

_____

_____

11 Rory describes what each family member at home is doing. Complete the chart below by describing what each family member is doing.

Family Member	What the Family Member is Doing
Rory	
Rory's mother	
Rory's father	

12 In what way is Rory motivated by his sister? Use at least **three** details from the passage in your answer.

END OF SET 5

PARCC Practice

Set 6

Long Informational Text

Instructions

This set has one passage for you to read. The passage is followed by questions.

Read each question carefully. For each multiple-choice question, fill in the circle for the correct answer. For other types of questions, follow the instructions given. Some of the questions require a written answer. Write your answer on the lines provided.

The Sahara Desert

The Sahara Desert is the world's largest subtropical desert. It covers most of North Africa. Its area is about 3.5 million square miles. This makes it almost as large as the United States of America. The Sahara Desert stretches all the way across Africa.

The Sahara Desert divides the continent of Africa into north and south. The southern border is marked by a savannah known as the Sahel. The land that lies to the south of the savannah is lush with more vegetation. The Sahara Desert features many large sand dunes. Some of these measure more than 600 feet from base to peak.

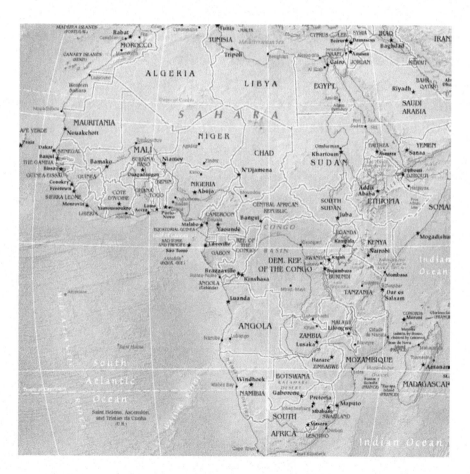

The Sahara Desert has been largely dry and with little plant life for more than 5,000 years. Before this time, it was far wetter than it is today. This allowed more plant life to thrive across its land. Thousands of ancient engravings have been found that show many types of river animals have lived in the Sahara Desert. These have been found mainly in southeast Algeria. These suggest that crocodiles lived in the region at some point in time.

The climate of the Sahara Desert has changed over several thousands of years. The area is also far smaller than it was during the last ice age. It was the end of the last ice age that brought a high level of rainfall to the Sahara. This was between 8000 and 6000 BC. Since this time, the northern part of the Sahara has gradually dried out. Though the southern Sahara still receives rain during monsoon season, it is still far less than years before. Some of the tallest mountain ranges occasionally receive snow peaks. The Tibetsi Mountains record some level of snowfall about once every seven years.

The modern era has seen several developments for the Sahara. One of these is that mines have been built to get the most from the natural resources within the region. There are also plans to build several highways across the Sahara. It is expected that one of these may be completed at some point in the future.

1   Read this sentence from the passage.

The Sahara Desert stretches all the way across Africa.

Why does the author most likely use the phrase "stretches all the way across"?

- Ⓐ   To emphasize how wide the desert is
- Ⓑ   To suggest that the desert is always changing
- Ⓒ   To show that the desert is mainly flat
- Ⓓ   To indicate that the desert has always been there

2   Read this sentence from the passage.

The land that lies to the south of the savannah is lush with more vegetation.

Explain how the word <u>lush</u> helps you imagine the savannah.

_____

_____

_____

_____

_____

3 Which sentence from the passage is best supported by the map?

Ⓐ The Sahara Desert is the world's largest subtropical desert.

Ⓑ The Sahara Desert stretches all the way across Africa.

Ⓒ The Sahara Desert features many large sand dunes.

Ⓓ The Sahara Desert has been largely dry and with little plant life for more than 5,000 years.

4 According to the passage, how was the Sahara Desert different thousands of years ago?

Ⓐ It had fewer animals.

Ⓑ It was wetter.

Ⓒ It had smaller sand dunes.

Ⓓ It was home to fewer people.

5 Which of the following is most similar about the Sahara Desert and the United States?

Ⓐ Its size

Ⓑ Its climate

Ⓒ Its uses

Ⓓ Its location

6 Where would this passage most likely be found?

- Ⓐ In an encyclopedia
- Ⓑ In an atlas
- Ⓒ In a history textbook
- Ⓓ In a book of short stories

7 How is the fourth paragraph of the passage organized?

- Ⓐ A problem is described and then a solution is given.
- Ⓑ The cause of an event is described.
- Ⓒ A claim is made and then details are given to support it.
- Ⓓ A question is asked and then answered.

8 Use the map to list **four** countries that are part of the Sahara Desert.

```
┌──────────┐                    ┌──────────┐
│          │                    │          │
└────────┬─┘                    └─┬────────┘
         └──┐   ┌────────────┐  ┌─┘
            └───│ Countries of│──┘
            ┌───│  the Sahara │──┐
         ┌──┘   └────────────┘  └─┐
┌────────┴─┐                    ┌─┴────────┐
│          │                    │          │
└──────────┘                    └──────────┘
```

9 Which sentence from the paragraph would make the best caption for the photograph?

- Ⓐ *The Sahara Desert stretches all the way across Africa.*
- Ⓑ *The Sahara Desert divides the continent of Africa into north and south.*
- Ⓒ *The Sahara Desert features many large sand dunes.*
- Ⓓ *The climate of the Sahara Desert has changed over several thousands of years.*

10 Do you think the Sahara Desert will stay the same in the future? Explain why or why not. Use details from the passage in your answer.

_____

_____

_____

_____

_____

11 Describe **three** interesting or surprising details about the Sahara Desert that are included in the passage. Explain what makes each detail interesting or surprising.

Detail	Why It's Interesting or Surprising

12 Even though life in the Sahara Desert is difficult, people do still live there. Describe **three** things that would make life in the Sahara Desert difficult. Use details from the passage in your answer.

END OF SET 6

PARCC Practice

Set 7

Paired Literary Passages

Instructions

This set has two short passages for you to read. Read each passage and answer the questions that follow it.

For each multiple-choice question, fill in the circle for the correct answer. For other types of questions, follow the instructions given. Some of the questions require a written answer. Write your answer on the lines provided.

After reading both passages, you will use information from both passages to answer a question. Write your answer on the lines provided.

Disappearing Dessert

It was a windy autumn morning in the backstreets of Brooklyn, New York. Tony was walking to the barber shop carrying a brown paper bag filled with cannolis. Along the way, he stopped to talk with Vinnie at the newspaper stand and gave him a few cannolis. Tony said his goodbyes and continued on toward the barber shop.

He had nearly arrived when he ran into Jen. The two spoke for a while and Tony gave Jen a handful of cannolis to eat for dessert that evening. Just around the corner from the barber shop, he saw Mr. Jackson walking his dog. He raced over to say hello, and then offered Mr. Jackson a cannoli.

Tony finally made it to the barber shop.

"Uncle Benny! Here are the delicious cannolis you asked Mamma to make for you!" Tony exclaimed.

He handed over the brown paper bag to his Uncle Benny and left the shop to go back home. Uncle Benny looked into the bag to find nothing inside.

"Crazy boy, there are no cannolis in here," he grumbled.

©John Mueller

1. Which detail from the passage best shows that Tony is generous?
   - Ⓐ He stops to talk to everyone he knows.
   - Ⓑ He offers to give everyone cannolis.
   - Ⓒ Uncle Benny calls him a crazy boy.
   - Ⓓ He bakes cannolis for his friends.

2. Who is telling the story?
   - Ⓐ Tony
   - Ⓑ Uncle Benny
   - Ⓒ Mr. Jackson
   - Ⓓ An outside narrator

3. What happened to the cannolis?
   - Ⓐ Tony gave them away.
   - Ⓑ They fell out of the bag.
   - Ⓒ Mamma didn't put any in the bag.
   - Ⓓ Tony ate them as he was walking.

4. What information does the photograph offer the reader?
   - Ⓐ It shows how many cannolis Tony had.
   - Ⓑ It shows why Uncle Benny asked for cannolis.
   - Ⓒ It shows what a cannoli is.
   - Ⓓ It shows what happened to the cannolis.

5   Do you think the passage is meant to be serious or humorous? Use details from the passage to explain your answer.

_____

_____

_____

_____

_____

6   Complete the summary of the main events of the passage.

Tony leaves home with a bag of cannolis.
Uncle Benny complains that there are no cannolis in the bag.

The Cookie Thief

Max was sitting at his desk early one morning flipping wildly through the pages of his notebook and pinning up hastily written notes on his corkboard. Max had covered his entire corkboard with clues, and drawn maps of his house. He paced back and forth, stared at the board, and then remembered something else. He scribbled something on another piece of note paper and added it to the board.

"I'm going to find out who ate my cookies if it's the last thing I do!" Max said as he worked away on his investigation. Max's dog Lucky just stared up at him.

Max jumped up and headed for his sister's room. Along with his father, she was the main suspect. Before he had even set foot outside of his room, Max tripped on something, stumbled, and fell. Max sat up and shook himself off. He looked around to see what he had tripped on. Right in front of him was a plastic bowl filled with cookie crumbs. Max suddenly remembered that he'd snuck out in the middle of the night for a snack. He was suddenly glad that he hadn't stormed in and blamed his sister.

7   Read this statement from the passage.

I'm going to find out who ate my cookies if it's the last thing I do!

Which literary device does Max use in this statement?

Ⓐ   Imagery, using details to create an image or picture

Ⓑ   Hyperbole, using exaggeration to make a point

Ⓒ   Simile, comparing two items using the words "like" or "as"

Ⓓ   Symbolism, using an object to stand for something else

8   What happens right after Max sees the bowl of cookie crumbs?
Ⓐ   He trips over something.
Ⓑ   He decides that his sister is to blame.
Ⓒ   He remembers how he snacked the night before.
Ⓓ   He starts to investigate the missing cookies.

9   Who is responsible for the missing cookies?
Ⓐ   Max
Ⓑ   Lucky
Ⓒ   Max's father
Ⓓ   Max's sister

10 How does Max feel at the start of the passage? How does Max feel at the end of the passage? Use details from the passage to support your answer.

_____

_____

_____

_____

11 How does the author create a sense of panic in the first paragraph? In your answer, identify at least **three** words or phrases the author uses to create a sense of panic.

_____

_____

_____

_____

12. Think about how Tony and Max both make a mistake. Do they each realize their mistake? Explain how this affects how each passage ends. Use details from both passages in your answer.

END OF SET 7

PARCC Practice

Set 8

Literary Analysis Task

Instructions

This set has two passages for you to read. Read each passage and answer the questions that follow it.

For each multiple-choice question, fill in the circle for the correct answer. For other types of questions, follow the instructions given. Some of the questions require a written answer. Write your answer on the lines provided.

After reading both passages, you will answer an essay question. You will use information from both passages to answer this question. Write your answer on the lines provided.

Haunted House

Marvin refused to believe in ghosts. Even on Halloween, he would not get scared when his friends Steven and Jason shared horror stories. They would gather in his bedroom and sit in pale lamplight talking about ghosts and goblins. The scary stories only made Marvin laugh.

One night they were at Marvin's house enjoying a sleepover. His friends decided to test how scared of ghosts Marvin really was.

"After he has fallen asleep, let's play a trick on him," said his best friend Steven.

"That's a great idea," Jason replied.

Just after midnight, Marvin drifted off to sleep. Steven and Jason looked at each other and nodded. Steven slipped out of his sleeping bag and hid in Marvin's closet. Jason lay still next to his friend and pretended to be asleep. After a moment Steven began to tap gently on the closet door. Marvin stirred gently. Then Steven continued and tapped even harder from behind the door. Marvin sprang from his sleep and sat upright. As the noise continued, he struggled to understand where it was coming from.

"Jason," he whispered. "Do you hear that sound?"

Jason pretended to wake from a deep sleep.

"What's wrong Marvin?" he asked.

"Do you hear that noise?" Marvin asked again.

Jason struggled to keep a smile off his face.

"Yes," Jason replied nervously. "I think it's coming from behind the closet door."

Marvin gulped as fear gripped his body. He climbed from his bed and stepped towards the closet. He began to freeze up as he got closer to the door. His trembling hand reached out towards the door. Just as he was about to push the door open, Steven leapt out from behind the door and shouted loudly. Marvin shrieked, jumped backwards, and fell onto the sleeping bags.

"Do you believe in ghosts now?" Jason asked with a giggle.

Marvin shook his head. He tried to look annoyed, but he couldn't help smiling. Steven was laughing out loud as he sat on a nearby chair. Marvin started to laugh as well.

"Of course he does," Steven said. "But I bet he didn't expect his own house to be haunted!"

"Fine, you got me," Marvin admitted. "For just a minute, I was scared. Nice one guys. Now let's get some sleep. And no more tricking."

Steven and Jason both promised they were done with tricking. But Marvin decided to leave the lamp on just in case.

1. In the sentence below, the word <u>pale</u> shows that the light was –

   They would gather in his bedroom and sit in pale lamplight talking about ghosts and goblins.

   Ⓐ bright

   Ⓑ clear

   Ⓒ dim

   Ⓓ warm

2. What does the photograph of Marvin at the start of the passage mainly suggest about him?

   Ⓐ He is not afraid of anything.

   Ⓑ He is known for playing jokes.

   Ⓒ He is more scared than he admits.

   Ⓓ He is about to have a prank played on him.

3. Place the events from the passage in order by writing the numbers 1, 2, 3, and 4 in front of each sentence.

   ___ Steven hides in the closet.

   ___ Marvin falls asleep.

   ___ Steven suggests playing a trick.

   ___ Jason asks Marvin if he believes in ghosts.

4 Read this sentence from the passage.

> **Just after midnight, Marvin drifted off to sleep.**

What mood does the phrase "drifted off" create?

- Ⓐ Curious
- Ⓑ Calm
- Ⓒ Playful
- Ⓓ Hopeful

5 Circle **three** words the author uses in paragraph 12 to emphasize how scared Marvin felt.

gulped	gripped	climbed	stepped
closet	trembling	reached	leapt

6 Describe the role that Steven and Jason play during the trick.

Steven:

_____

_____

Jason:

_____

_____

7 Why does Marvin jump backwards and fall onto the sleeping bags?

- Ⓐ Steven pushes him.
- Ⓑ Steven scares him.
- Ⓒ He is angry with Steven.
- Ⓓ He wants to go back to sleep.

8 Why does the author most likely use the word <u>sprang</u> instead of <u>woke</u> in the sentence below?

Marvin sprang from his sleep and sat upright.

- Ⓐ To show that Marvin knows about the trick
- Ⓑ To show that Marvin feels sleepy
- Ⓒ To show that Marvin had a bad dream
- Ⓓ To show that Marvin woke suddenly

9 After Marvin hears a noise, the author says that Jason "struggled to keep a smile off his face." Explain why Jason has to stop himself from smiling.

_____

_____

_____

_____

_____

10 Choose **two** sentences from the paragraph below that create suspense. Circle the **two** sentences below. Then explain why you chose those sentences.

> Marvin gulped as fear gripped his body. He climbed from his bed and stepped towards the closet. He began to freeze up as he got closer to the door. His trembling hand reached out towards the door. Just as he was about to push the door open, Steven leapt out from behind the door and shouted loudly. Marvin shrieked, jumped backwards, and fell onto the sleeping bags.

_____

_____

_____

_____

_____

_____

11 Do you think the trick that Steven and Jason played was mean or funny? Use details from the passage to support your opinion.

_____

_____

_____

_____

_____

12 Think about how Marvin seems to feel about the trick. Circle the sentence that describes how you think he feels about the trick.

     It was mean.   It was funny.

Give **two** details that help show whether he thinks the trick was mean or funny.

1: _____

_____

2: _____

_____

Beneath the Silver Stars

It was fair to say that Lucas was sometimes mean to his younger sister. He would often play practical jokes on her. His parents used to tell him that it wasn't nice to scare her. He would always say that he never meant to upset her and that he was just joking. The situation was worse when the family went camping together. Lucas would play all sorts of tricks on his sister once the sun had gone down. On one particular trip, his sister Molly was having breakfast and talking about her brother to their dad.

"Why won't he just stop playing his silly pranks?" Molly complained.

"He's just a boy," her father replied. "Although, we could get him back if you want to."

Molly raised her eyebrows. Then a smile came to her face.

"How do you mean, Dad?" she asked.

"Well, I think we should play some tricks of our own," he replied. "After all, it's just a little harmless fun. We should wait until tonight and play a few little games."

Molly was very excited at her father's suggestion and thought it was a great idea.

"We won't scare him too much will we?" she asked.

"Not at all," replied her father. "When I was a child my brother used to play tricks on me all the time. It is just something that people do, darling."

By 10 o'clock that evening, it was very dark. All of the family had gone to bed. Molly's mother was fast asleep and her father was awake but quiet in his tent. At about 11 o'clock he began to hear noises from outside of the tent. He undid the zip and peered out into the darkness. He could see Lucas making howling noises from just outside Molly's tent. He chuckled softly to himself and crept slowly out onto the grass. As Lucas continued to howl, his father made his way across and hid behind a nearby tree. Lucas then paused and began to edge closer to Molly's tent. As he did so his father let out a high-pitched howl at the very top of his voice.

Lucas stood completely still. He half turned but did not want to see what was behind him. His knees started shaking a little. His father began to creep up behind him. By now Molly was peeking out of a small gap in her tent. Lucas stared ahead of him and thought about running back to his tent. As he was about to do so, his father reached out and touched his shoulder.

Lucas leapt from the spot and ran towards his tent. Molly laughed loudly as Lucas raced away.

"You see," Molly's father said with a chuckle. "Now wasn't that fun?"

13 If the passage was given another title, which title would best fit?

  Ⓐ Family Fights

  Ⓑ Payback Time

  Ⓒ How to Camp

  Ⓓ Good Times

14 Explain why you chose the title in Question 13. In your answer, describe how the title you chose tells what the passage is about.

_____

_____

_____

_____

_____

15 When the father suggests getting Lucas back, the author states that Molly "raised her eyebrows." The author describes this to show that Molly is –

  Ⓐ confused

  Ⓑ frightened

  Ⓒ interested

  Ⓓ amused

16 Circle the **two** words from the passage that have about the same meaning.

fair	pranks	harmless
chuckled	mean	peeking
tricks	scare	running

17 Why does Lucas most likely make howling noises outside Molly's tent?

    Ⓐ   He is trying to scare Molly.

    Ⓑ   He wants Molly to come outside.

    Ⓒ   He knows that Molly is going to play a trick on him.

    Ⓓ   He is trying to keep animals away from the area.

18 How is the passage mainly organized?

    Ⓐ   Two events are compared and contrasted.

    Ⓑ   Events are described in the order they occur.

    Ⓒ   Facts are given to support an argument.

    Ⓓ   A question is asked and then answered.

19   Which sentence from the passage best shows that Molly cares about her brother?

   Ⓐ   *"Why won't he just stop playing his silly pranks?" Molly complained.*

   Ⓑ   *Molly was very excited at her father's suggestion and thought it was a great idea.*

   Ⓒ   *"We won't scare him too much will we?" she asked.*

   Ⓓ   *Molly laughed loudly as Lucas raced away.*

20   Complete the web below by adding **three** more details that show that Lucas was scared when he heard his father's high-pitched howl.

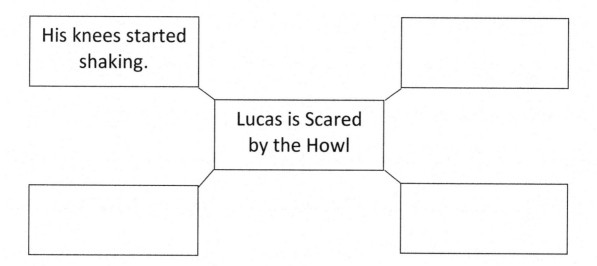

21   Which of these best explains the humor in the story?
   Ⓐ   Molly is tired of her brother playing tricks on her.
   Ⓑ   Molly and her family are trying to have a fun camping trip.
   Ⓒ   Lucas does not really want to upset his sister.
   Ⓓ   Lucas is scared by his father while he is trying to scare his sister.

22 Give **two** reasons that Molly decided to play a trick on Lucas.

1: _____

_____

2: _____

_____

23 Do you think Molly's trick will stop Lucas from playing tricks in the future? Explain why or why not.

_____

_____

_____

_____

_____

24 You have read two passages about people playing tricks. Write an essay that compares the two tricks played.

- In your answer, tell who plays the trick and why the trick is played.
- Explain how each trick involves scaring someone.
- Use details from both passages to support your answer.

END OF SET 8

PARCC Practice

Set 9

Research Simulation Task

Instructions

This set has three passages for you to read. Read each passage and answer the questions that follow it.

For each multiple-choice question, fill in the circle for the correct answer. For other types of questions, follow the instructions given. Some of the questions require a written answer. Write your answer on the lines provided.

After reading the three passages, you will answer an essay question. You will use information from all three passages to answer this question. Write your answer on the lines provided.

Happy Campers Summer Retreat

As a parent, your child's happiness is the most important thing to you. It is important to keep children healthy and active. This can be difficult to achieve. After all, many people have busy careers as well. The Happy Campers Summer Retreat was developed to help parents with this challenge.

Michael Gibson founded our group in 1998. We run a summer camp for children during the holidays. We are open from May to September. We look after hundreds of children every single year. Our staff are all experienced and fully-trained. The camp is based in the Colorado Mountains. It offers a wide range of activities for children. Our group's mission is to create a new generation of active children across America.

Our program helps children in a number of ways. It will help develop all of the qualities listed below.
- Physical fitness
- Problem-solving skills
- Social skills
- Sports ability and experience

The Happy Campers Summer Retreat can benefit all children. Some children are good at school, but rarely active. Our program will help encourage an interest in sports. Other children are mainly interested in sports. These children will play sports, but will also learn new skills. Team sports are also very important. They are used to help children develop teamwork skills, social skills, and communication skills. Children will also have the chance to try new activities. Our program is designed to help develop a complete and fully active child.

Our program is very affordable. It is available to any family in America. Your child's stay can be as short as a week or as long as six weeks. We will also cater to any special needs that your child may have.

Why not call us today or send us an email with your enquiry? Take action now and give your child this great opportunity! Our helpful staff will be able to give you all of the answers that you need.

1. In the sentence below, what does the word <u>affordable</u> refer to?

   Our program is very affordable.

   Ⓐ How easy the program is

   Ⓑ How much the program costs

   Ⓒ How the program benefits children

   Ⓓ How active children need to be

2. According to the passage, where is the summer retreat held?

   Ⓐ Lake Michigan

   Ⓑ Colorado Mountains

   Ⓒ Yosemite National Park

   Ⓓ Venice Beach

3. Which word best describes how the author of the passage sounds?

   Ⓐ Serious and determined

   Ⓑ Concerned and fearful

   Ⓒ Positive and encouraging

   Ⓓ Lighthearted and funny

4 Who is the passage mainly written to appeal to?

    Ⓐ   Parents

    Ⓑ   Teachers

    Ⓒ   Students

    Ⓓ   Sports people

5 Think about your answer to Question 4. Choose **two** paragraphs that best support your answer. Circle the paragraphs below. Then explain how each paragraph supports your answer.

    Paragraph: 1   2   3   4   5   6

First paragraph selected:

_____

_____

Second paragraph selected:

_____

_____

6   Look at the web below.

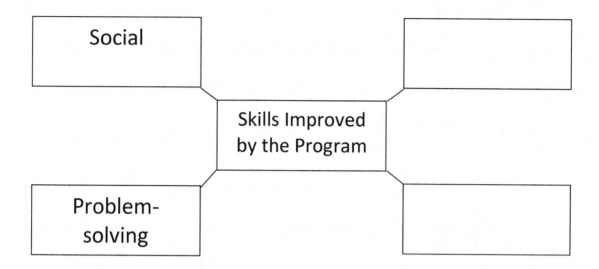

Which of these best completes the web? Write the **two** best answers in the web.

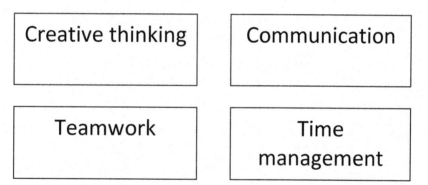

7   The passage was probably written mainly to –

  Ⓐ   encourage parents to send their children to the camp

  Ⓑ   compare the camp with other activities

  Ⓒ   describe the history of the camp

  Ⓓ   inform parents about the benefits of outdoor activities

8   Which sentence is included mainly to persuade the reader?

   Ⓐ   *After all, many people have busy careers as well.*

   Ⓑ   *We run a summer camp for children during the holidays.*

   Ⓒ   *It is available to any family in America.*

   Ⓓ   *Take action now and give your child this great opportunity!*

9   Choose the **two** sentences from the second paragraph that best support the idea that parents can trust the camp. Tick **two** boxes below to show your choices.

   ☐   *Michael Gibson founded our group in 1998.*

   ☐   *We run a summer camp for children during the holidays.*

   ☐   *We are open from May to September.*

   ☐   *We look after hundreds of children every single year.*

   ☐   *Our staff are all experienced and fully-trained.*

   ☐   *The camp is based in the Colorado Mountains.*

   ☐   *It offers a wide range of activities for children.*

   ☐   *Our group's mission is to create a new generation of active children across America.*

The West Moor Sports Camp

The health of our children is important. Good health means eating well and being active. Children should take part in sports or other activities often. This isn't always easy. In cities, it can be hard to find activities to do. Don't be alarmed, though. The West Moor Sports Camp can help!

The West Moor Sports Camp is an outdoor camp for people of all ages. Children can enjoy outdoor activities. They can also make new friends. All while the parents relax, knowing that their children are safe.

The West Moor Sports Camp is located among lush fields. There is a lot of open space for youngsters to run around and enjoy themselves. There are many games and sports that they can take part in. These include football, soccer, baseball, basketball, athletics, and tennis. They can also take part in activities on the lake like rowing and sailing. There are also fitness classes that children can take part in.

There are many benefits to the camp. The first is that children will take part in a fitness program that they will enjoy! They will become fitter while having fun! The second is that children will make new friends. They will learn how to work with other children. It may also help children develop good fitness habits. Finally, children will have the chance to try activities they might never have been able to do before. Children can have a go at everything. With so many to choose from, they might find the sport or hobby that is just right for them.

Many children find that they enjoy playing sports. They leave our camp with a new appreciation for being outdoors and being active. It becomes a new interest. In the age of computer games, this is a great thing!

So visit our website today to find out more. Give your children a better future!

10 Read this sentence from the passage.

In cities, it can be hard to find activities to do.

Which word means the opposite of hard?
- Ⓐ   Cheap
- Ⓑ   Difficult
- Ⓒ   Easy
- Ⓓ   Costly

11 In the first paragraph, what does the word alarmed mean?
- Ⓐ   Worried
- Ⓑ   Lazy
- Ⓒ   Confused
- Ⓓ   Silly

12 How is the first paragraph mainly organized?
- Ⓐ   A problem is described and then a solution is given.
- Ⓑ   Events are described in the order they occur.
- Ⓒ   Facts are given to support an argument.
- Ⓓ   A question is asked and then answered.

13 The first paragraph states that children "should take part in sports or other activities often." How does the camp encourage children to do this? Use at least **two** details from the passage in your answer.

_____

_____

_____

_____

_____

14 Use details from the passage to complete the web below.

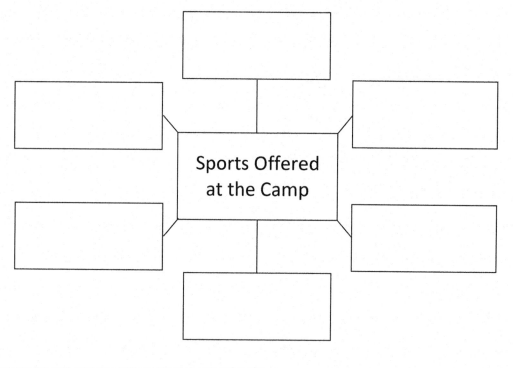

15   The photograph is probably included mainly as an example of children –
   Ⓐ   being looked after
   Ⓑ   making new friends
   Ⓒ   solving problems
   Ⓓ   working together

16   Which question is the passage mainly intended to answer?
   Ⓐ   When was the West Moor Sports Camp started?
   Ⓑ   What skills do young people need to develop?
   Ⓒ   Why should children attend the West Moor Sports Camp?
   Ⓓ   Will the West Moor Sports Camp be safe for kids?

17   According to the passage, what should you do to find out more about the camp?
   Ⓐ   Request a brochure
   Ⓑ   Telephone the camp
   Ⓒ   Attend an open day
   Ⓓ   Visit the camp's website

18 Look at the diagram below. Complete the diagram by listing **two** more benefits of the camp.

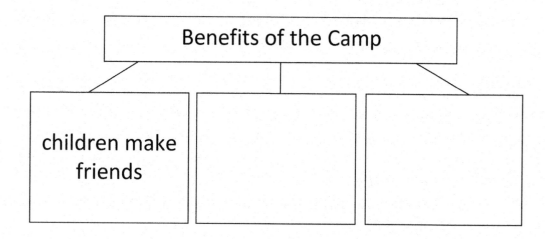

19 Is the information given about the camp biased toward making the camp sound good? Explain your answer.

_____

_____

_____

_____

_____

_____

Be Prepared

The Scouts is a worldwide youth movement aimed at supporting the physical and mental development of young males. The Scouts was started in 1907 by Robert Baden-Powell, who was a Lieutenant General in the British Army.

During the 1900s, the movement grew to include three different age groups of boys. The Cub Scouts is for boys aged from 7 to 11. The Scouts is for boys aged 11 to 18. The Rover Scouts is for boys aged over 18. In 1910, a similar organization was created for girls. It is known as the Girl Guides. The motto of the Scouts is "Be Prepared." The aim of the Scouts is not just to promote fitness, but to build character. By taking part in a range of activities, members learn important personal skills.

One of the key features of the Scouts is that members earn merit badges as they develop new skills. Some of the badges that can be earned are shown below. Once each badge is earned, the patch for the badge can be added to the uniform.

Bird Study, Fire Safety, Plant Science, Rowing, First Aid, Cooking, Camping, and Public Speaking are just some of the badges that can be earned.

In 1911, an official handbook for the Boy Scouts of America was published. This introduction to the book encourages readers to join the scouts.

> "Scout" used to mean the one on watch for the rest. We have widened the word a little. We have made it fit the town as well as the wilderness and suited it to peace time instead of war. We have made the scout an expert in Life-craft as well as Wood-craft, for he is trained in the things of the heart as well as head and hand. Scouting we have made to cover riding, swimming, tramping, trailing, photography, first aid, camping, handicraft, loyalty, obedience, courtesy, thrift, courage, and kindness.
>
> Do these things appeal to you? Do you love the woods? Do you wish to learn the trees as the forester knows them? And the stars not as an astronomer, but as a traveler?
>
> Do you wish to have all-round, well-developed muscles, not those of a great athlete, but those of a sound body that will not fail you? Would you like to be an expert camper who can always make himself comfortable out of doors, and a swimmer that fears no waters? Do you desire the knowledge to help the wounded quickly, and to make yourself cool and self-reliant in an emergency?
>
> Do you believe in loyalty, courage, and kindness? Would you like to form habits that will surely make your success in life?
>
> Then, whether you be farm boy or shoe clerk, newsboy or millionaire's son, your place is in our ranks, for these are the thoughts in scouting. It will help you to do better work with your pigs, your shoes, your papers, or your dollars. It will give you new pleasures in life. It will teach you so much of the outdoor world that you wish to know.

Even though this introduction was written over one hundred years ago, it still describes what the Scouts are about today. It is about learning a wide range of skills that will prepare you for all kinds of situations. You will learn new things, experience new things, and have the kinds of abilities that will serve you well throughout your life.

20 Complete the table below using information from the passage.

Age Groups for Boys

Group	Age

21 If the author added another paragraph to the end of the passage, what would it be most likely to describe?

    Ⓐ   What Robert Baden-Powell's childhood was like

    Ⓑ   Who started the Girl Guides

    Ⓒ   What activities the Scouts do

    Ⓓ   How to join the Scouts

22 Which word could best be used in place of <u>worldwide</u> in the first sentence?

    Ⓐ   Local

    Ⓑ   Important

    Ⓒ   International

    Ⓓ   Experienced

23 What do the examples of the badges shown best show about being a Scout?

- Ⓐ You will need to be fit and healthy.
- Ⓑ You will mainly learn how to help others.
- Ⓒ You will get to do a range of different things.
- Ⓓ You will have to work hard to earn each badge.

24 The introduction to the handbook tries to get young readers interested in becoming a Scout. Describe at least **two** ways the author tries to do this. Then explain whether you think the author is successful.

_____

_____

_____

_____

_____

_____

_____

_____

_____

25 You have read three passages that encourage people to go to camps or join groups that encourage being active. Write an article for your school newspaper encouraging students to go to a camp or join a group like the Scouts.

- In your article, describe the benefits of going to a camp or joining a group like the Scouts.
- Explain what students can gain from these activities.

END OF SET 9

PARCC Practice

Set 10

Narrative Writing Task

Instructions

This set has one passage for you to read. The passage is followed by questions.

Read each question carefully. For each multiple-choice question, fill in the circle for the correct answer. For other types of questions, follow the instructions given. Some of the questions require a written answer. Write your answer on the lines provided.

The last question requires you to write a story. Write your answer on the lines provided.

The Taming of the Lion

The lion had a fearful roar
that scared all who dared to follow.
It made his victims run and hide,
and pray for their tomorrow.

His mane was as glorious as sunshine,
and framed his handsome face.
His lair was known to all around
as a truly frightening place.

Until he met a maiden,
and fell hopelessly in love.
His roar became a whisper,
a soft sound to birds above.

His lair was soon a palace,
a kindly home of gentle calm,
where he would hold his loved ones,
and make sure they met no harm.

The lion never harmed another,
or chased his worried prey.
Instead they lived in harmony
and shared each summer's day.

He had been tamed within an instant
by the gentle hand of love,
that would keep him calm forever
beneath the flight of gentle doves.

1   Read this line from the poem.

The lion had a fearful roar

What does the word <u>fearful</u> mean?

- Ⓐ   Without fear
- Ⓑ   Having fear
- Ⓒ   More fear
- Ⓓ   Less fear

2   According to the poem, why does the lion become tamer?

- Ⓐ   He gets older.
- Ⓑ   He falls in love.
- Ⓒ   He has children.
- Ⓓ   He starts feeling lonely.

3   What is the rhyme pattern of each stanza of the poem?

- Ⓐ   The second and fourth lines rhyme.
- Ⓑ   There are two pairs of rhyming lines.
- Ⓒ   The first and last lines rhyme.
- Ⓓ   None of the lines rhyme.

4 Select the line from the poem that contains a simile.

☐ *The lion had a fearful roar*

☐ *that scared all who dared to follow.*

☐ *It made his victims run and hide,*

☐ *and pray for their tomorrow.*

☐ *His mane was as glorious as sunshine,*

☐ *and framed his handsome face.*

☐ *His lair was known to all around*

☐ *as a truly frightening place.*

5 Describe the meaning of the simile identified in Question 4. In your answer, explain what the simile helps you imagine.

_____

_____

_____

_____

_____

6 Which word best describes the tone of the poem?

  Ⓐ Funny

  Ⓑ Serious

  Ⓒ Sweet

  Ⓓ Tense

7 Read this line from the poem.

  a soft sound to birds above

  The alliteration in this line mainly creates a feeling of —

  Ⓐ uneasiness

  Ⓑ surprise

  Ⓒ calm

  Ⓓ fear

8 The poem states that the lion had been tamed "within an instant." What does the phrase "within an instant" mean?

  Ⓐ Very well

  Ⓑ Unusually

  Ⓒ Suddenly

  Ⓓ Over a long time

9   Read this line from the poem.

   His roar became a whisper,

   What does this change show about the lion?

   Ⓐ   He has become shy.

   Ⓑ   He is no longer scary.

   Ⓒ   He feels afraid.

   Ⓓ   He listens to others.

10   What does the imagery in the lines below help the reader understand?

   **It made his victims run and hide,
   and pray for their tomorrow.**

   Ⓐ   Where the lion lives

   Ⓑ   How feared the lion is

   Ⓒ   Why the lion dislikes people

   Ⓓ   How strong and fast the lion is

11   How many stanzas does the poem have? Circle the correct answer.

   2   3   4   6   8   12   20   24

12. Which pair of lines from the poem explain what causes the lion to change?

   Ⓐ *His mane was as glorious as sunshine,*
   and framed his handsome face.

   Ⓑ *Until he met a maiden,*
   and fell hopelessly in love.

   Ⓒ *His lair was soon a palace,*
   a kindly home of gentle calm,

   Ⓓ *The lion never harmed another,*
   or chased his worried prey.

13. Compare the language used to describe the lion at the start of the poem with the language used at the end of the poem. Complete the table below by listing **three** more examples of words or phrases the poet uses to show what the lion is like before and after he changes.

Words to Show the Lion is Feared	Words to Show the Lion is Harmless
dared to follow	palace
victims	gentle calm

14 In the poem, the lion changes when he meets a maiden and falls in love. Think about how the people would feel now that they no longer have to fear the lion. Write a story that tells about the events from the point of view of the people. In your story, describe how the lion was once feared but is no longer feared.

END OF SET 10

PARCC Practice

Set 11

Short Informational Text

Instructions

This set has one passage for you to read. The passage is followed by questions.

Read each question carefully. For each multiple-choice question, fill in the circle for the correct answer. For other types of questions, follow the instructions given. Some of the questions require a written answer. Write your answer on the lines provided.

Grooming a King Charles Cavalier

The King Charles Cavalier is a small breed of Spaniel dog. It is known as a toy dog by kennel clubs. They are very popular in the United States and around the world. These dogs have a silky coat and can be difficult to groom. Professional groomers can carry out the task. However, many owners choose to save money and groom their dog themselves. It takes some patience, but you can learn to groom a King Charles Cavalier.

Start by making sure you have the correct equipment to groom your dog correctly. You will need:
- a comb
- a brush
- dog-friendly conditioner

You should complete these steps when your dog is clean. If your dog's coat is dirty, give the dog a bath first. Then dry the coat before starting.

Step 1
Before you start, make sure that your dog is in a comfortable position either on your lap or on a blanket. Your dog should be nice and relaxed.

Step 2
Take your comb and move it smoothly through the coat. There may be some knots or tangles, so be sure not to comb it too fast. You don't want to pull at the dog's fur, cause your dog any discomfort, or scare it. Be gentle, but make sure that all dead or matted hair is removed.

Step 3
Once the combing is complete, add some of the conditioner to the coat. This will add shine and make it easier to brush your dog.

Step 4
Comb your dog's coat for a second time to make sure that it is as smooth as it can be.

Step 5
It is now time to brush your King Charles Cavalier. Hold the brush firmly in your hand and be sure to keep your dog still. Move the brush gently through your dog's coat. Take care to smooth out any lumps or patches of uneven hair. Move through each area of the coat twice.

Step 6
Once you've finished brushing, condition your dogs coat again. This helps to keep your dog's coat free from tangles. It will also make it easier to groom your dog in the future.

Step 7
Lastly, all you need to do is gently pat the dog's coat dry. Your dog is now nicely groomed and the coat should stay that way for around 4 to 6 weeks.

You can give your dog a small food reward after you've finished the grooming. This will help make sure your dog looks forward to being groomed.

1   Read this sentence from the passage.

> **Be gentle and make sure that all dead or matted hair is removed.**

Which word means the opposite of <u>gentle</u>?

- Ⓐ   Calm
- Ⓑ   Fast
- Ⓒ   Rough
- Ⓓ   Slow

2   In the sentence below, what does the word <u>silky</u> mainly describe?

> **These dogs have a silky coat and can be difficult to groom.**

- Ⓐ   How long the coat is
- Ⓑ   How the coat feels
- Ⓒ   What the coat smells like
- Ⓓ   What color the coat is

3   Circle **all** the steps that the conditioner is used.

Step 1   Step 2   Step 3   Step 4

Step 5   Step 6   Step 7

4 Describe **two** reasons it is important to comb the dog's coat slowly and carefully.

1: _____

_____

2: _____

_____

5 Select **all** the benefits of using conditioner. Tick the box for each benefit mentioned in the passage.

☐ To add shine to the coat

☐ To stop the coat from getting tangles

☐ To prevent the dog from getting fleas

☐ To remove dirt from the dog's coat

☐ To make it easier to brush the dog

☐ To help the dog relax

6 What is the main purpose of the passage?

　　Ⓐ　To teach readers how to do something

　　Ⓑ　To entertain readers with a story

　　Ⓒ　To inform readers about a type of dog

　　Ⓓ　To compare different types of dog products

7 What is the purpose of the bullet points?

　　Ⓐ　To describe the steps

　　Ⓑ　To give useful hints

　　Ⓒ　To list the items needed

　　Ⓓ　To highlight the key points

8 The first tip says to complete the steps when the dog is clean. Why do you think it is important that the dog is clean? In your answer, describe **two** problems you might have if the dog's coat is dirty.

_____

_____

_____

_____

_____

9 Which detail from the photograph is most relevant to the passage?

- Ⓐ The size of the dog
- Ⓑ The color of the dog
- Ⓒ The look of the dog's fur
- Ⓓ The look on the dog's face

10 According to the passage, what should you do right after brushing the dog?

- Ⓐ Comb the dog's coat a second time
- Ⓑ Condition the dog's coat
- Ⓒ Rinse the dog's coat
- Ⓓ Give the dog a treat

11 Complete the web below by listing **three** reasons to support the idea that it takes patience to groom a King Charles Cavalier.

```
        ┌─────────────────────────┐
        │ It takes patience to groom a │
        │   King Charles Cavalier.     │
        └─────────────────────────┘
         /          |          \
   ┌────────┐  ┌────────┐  ┌────────┐
   │        │  │        │  │        │
   │        │  │        │  │        │
   └────────┘  └────────┘  └────────┘
```

12 If you owned a King Charles Cavalier, would you groom it yourself or pay a professional to do it? Explain why you made that decision.

_____

_____

_____

_____

_____

_____

_____

_____

_____

_____

_____

_____

END OF SET 11

PARCC Practice

Set 12

Short Literary Text

Instructions

This set has one passage for you to read. The passage is followed by questions.

Read each question carefully. For each multiple-choice question, fill in the circle for the correct answer. For other types of questions, follow the instructions given. Some of the questions require a written answer. Write your answer on the lines provided.

Keep Smiling

Happiness is something special,
To be enjoyed by young and old,
And then be shared by one another,
To keep us warm through winter's cold.

Whatever time or season,
Or hour of the day,
Happiness can lift your spirits,
More than words could ever say.

And turn your sadness into joy,
Make a smile from a frown.
It brings a burst of gentle laughter,
And lifts you up when you are down.

Without it life is nothing,
Just a pale shade of gray.
An everlasting stretch of nighttime,
That waits patiently for day.

So make the most of living,
And make happiness your friend.
Greet it warmly and keep smiling,
Keep happiness close until your end.

And never doubt its power,
To bring enjoyment out of sorrow,
And leave you smiling through your slumber,
As you wait to greet tomorrow.

1 What does the word <u>sorrow</u> most likely mean in the line below?

   To bring enjoyment out of sorrow,

   Ⓐ   Boredom

   Ⓑ   Problems

   Ⓒ   Sadness

   Ⓓ   Peace

2 What does the line below mean?

   Happiness can lift your spirits,

   Ⓐ   Happiness can be hard to find.

   Ⓑ   Happiness can make you feel better.

   Ⓒ   Happiness can feel like floating.

   Ⓓ   Happiness can bring people closer.

3 Based on your answer to Question 2, choose **two** lines that have about the same meaning. Write the **two** lines you have chosen below.

   Line 1:

   _____

   Line 2:

   _____

4 The poet describes how life can be "just a pale shade of gray" to show that life can be –

- Ⓐ simple
- Ⓑ weird
- Ⓒ boring
- Ⓓ difficult

5 Read this line from the poem.

It brings a burst of gentle laughter,

Which literary technique does the poet use to help the reader imagine sudden laughter?

- Ⓐ Alliteration
- Ⓑ Simile
- Ⓒ Metaphor
- Ⓓ Flashback

6 What is the rhyme pattern of each stanza of the poem?

- Ⓐ All the lines rhyme with each other.
- Ⓑ There are two pairs of rhyming lines.
- Ⓒ The second and fourth lines rhyme.
- Ⓓ None of the lines rhyme.

7 What type of poem is "Keep Smiling"?

- Ⓐ Rhyming
- Ⓑ Free verse
- Ⓒ Limerick
- Ⓓ Sonnet

8 Which statement best describes the theme of the poem?

- Ⓐ You should have fun while you are young.
- Ⓑ Every day is a chance to try something new.
- Ⓒ It is important to be happy and enjoy life.
- Ⓓ There is no time like the present.

9 Hyperbole is the use of exaggeration to make a point. Which line from the poem contains hyperbole?

- Ⓐ *To be enjoyed by young and old,*
- Ⓑ *Make a smile from a frown.*
- Ⓒ *An everlasting stretch of nighttime,*
- Ⓓ *As you wait to greet tomorrow.*

10 The poet states that happiness can "keep us warm through winter's cold." Explain what the poet means by this.

_____

_____

_____

_____

_____

_____

11 The poet chose a field of flowers as the background photograph for the poem. Why do you think the poet chose this photograph? In your answer, explain how it relates to the theme or the tone of the poem.

_____

_____

_____

_____

_____

_____

12 Describe what the poem teaches you about happiness and sadness. In your answer, give **three** reasons it is important to keep smiling.

END OF SET 12

PARCC Practice

Set 13

Long Informational Text

Instructions

This set has one passage for you to read. The passage is followed by questions.

Read each question carefully. For each multiple-choice question, fill in the circle for the correct answer. For other types of questions, follow the instructions given. Some of the questions require a written answer. Write your answer on the lines provided.

Baseball

Baseball is a bat and ball sport that is very popular in America. It is a game played between two teams of nine players. The aim of the game is to score runs. Players strike the ball with a bat. Then they run around four bases. When they cross home base again, they have scored a run. Home base is also known as the home plate. The bases are set at each corner of a 90-foot square called the diamond.

Each team takes it in turns to bat while the other fields. The other team must stop the batters from scoring runs by getting them out. To get a batter out, they can strike them out. This means that the batter misses the ball three times. They can also get them out by catching the ball if the batter isn't safe on a base. Players can stop at any of the four bases once they have hit the ball, which makes them safe.

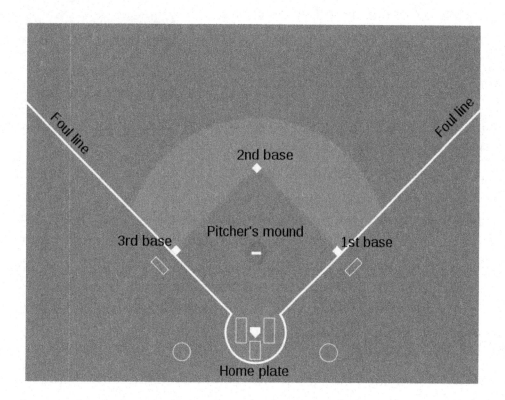

Once three players are out, the fielding team takes their turn to bat. Each time a team bats, it is known as an innings. There are nine innings in a professional league game. The team that scores the most runs at the close of all innings is the winner. The player who throws the ball to the batting team is known as the pitcher. Each professional game has at least two umpires who ensure fair play between the teams. Some big games have six umpires. There is one at each base and another two along the foul lines. The umpires know that their decisions could change the game, so they watch their areas closely.

The umpires judge whether players on the batting team are out or not. This usually means working out whether the player touched the base before the fielder touched the base with the ball. Umpires also decide whether or not pitchers throw the ball correctly. For example, a pitcher must have one foot on the pitcher's mound at the start of every pitch. The umpires also judge whether each pitch passes through the batter's strike zone. If the ball does pass through, the pitch will count as a strike even if the batter does not swing. If the ball is too high or too wide, it is counted as a ball.

The umpire watches closely. If the runner reaches the base before the fielder receives the ball, he will be safe and will not be out.

Baseball developed from the traditional bat and ball games of the 18th century. It has a sister sport referred to as rounders. Both of these sports were first played in America by British and Irish immigrants. It has since developed to become known as the national sport of North America. Over the last 20 years, the sport has also grown worldwide. It is now very popular in the Caribbean, South America, and many parts of Asia.

Baseball is a great sport for young kids. It is safer than contact sports like football. It requires a range of skills. Players can focus on being good batters, pitchers, or fielders. At the same time, players learn to work together as a team.

1. Read this sentence from the passage.

   Each professional game has at least two umpires who ensure fair play between the teams.

   Which meaning of the word <u>fair</u> is used in this sentence?
   - Ⓐ Average
   - Ⓑ Just or correct
   - Ⓒ Pale
   - Ⓓ Sunny or clear

2. What is the player who throws the ball to the batting team called?
   - Ⓐ Bowler
   - Ⓑ Runner
   - Ⓒ Catcher
   - Ⓓ Pitcher

3. Which sentence from the passage is an opinion?
   - Ⓐ *It is a game played between two teams of nine players.*
   - Ⓑ *Each time a team bats, it is known as an innings.*
   - Ⓒ *Over the last 20 years, the sport has also grown worldwide.*
   - Ⓓ *It is safer than contact sports like football.*

4 What does the diagram most help the reader understand?

    Ⓐ   How many players are on a team

    Ⓑ   The main rules of baseball

    Ⓒ   Where the bases are located

    Ⓓ   What the purpose of the pitcher is

5 Circle **all** the terms related to baseball that are explained in the passage.

platform	goal	home plate
diamond	coach	innings
tackle	net	strike zone

6 Choose **two** of the words you circled in Question 5. Write a definition of each word below.

Word: _____

Meaning: _____

_____

Word: _____

Meaning: _____

_____

7 The passage was probably written mainly to –

    Ⓐ   encourage people to play sport

    Ⓑ   teach readers about the sport of baseball

    Ⓒ   show why baseball is popular

    Ⓓ   describe the history of baseball

8 Read this sentence from the passage.

    Players strike the ball with a bat.

Which word could best be used in place of <u>strike</u>?

    Ⓐ   Swap

    Ⓑ   Shove

    Ⓒ   Hit

    Ⓓ   Throw

9 Complete the web below by listing **three** things the umpires judge.

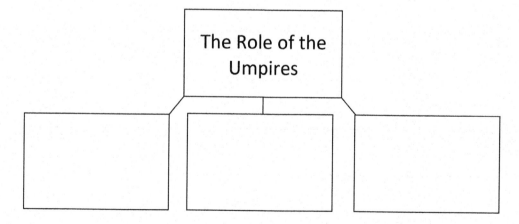

10 What is the main purpose of the information in paragraph 5? Describe how the purpose is different from the main purpose of the passage overall.

_____

_____

_____

_____

_____

11 How does the photograph help explain why an umpire is placed at each base in big games? Use details from the passage to support your answer.

_____

_____

_____

_____

_____

12 The author says that baseball is a "great sport for young kids." Do you agree with this? Use details from the passage to explain why or why not.

END OF SET 13

PARCC Practice

Set 14

Paired Informational Passages

Instructions

This set has two short passages for you to read. Read each passage and answer the questions that follow it.

For each multiple-choice question, fill in the circle for the correct answer. For other types of questions, follow the instructions given. Some of the questions require a written answer. Write your answer on the lines provided.

After reading both passages, you will use information from both passages to answer a question. Write your answer on the lines provided.

Mozart

Mozart is a famous German composer of the classical era. His full name was Wolfgang Amadeus Mozart and he was born in 1756. He has composed over 600 pieces of classical music. These include works for the piano and violin, as well as whole operas.

Mozart began composing at the age of 5. At this time, he wrote small pieces for his father. He continued to learn and write music all through his youth. When he was 17, he worked as a court musician in Austria. He was given the opportunity to write a range of musical pieces.

Mozart left Austria in search of better work, and lived in Paris for over a year. During this time, he was unable to find work, but he still continued writing music.

He then moved to Vienna. Mozart wrote most of his best-known work while living in Vienna. He wrote operas, performed in concerts, produced concerts, and performed solos. He gained both money and fame and was able to live very well for a short time. However, he lived too lavishly and his income could not keep up with his spending. Much of his later years were spent struggling to support his family and to pay off his debts. He died at the age of 35 in 1791.

As well as his major works, he is remembered for inspiring later composers. Other famous composers including Beethoven and Hummel studied his work and learned from it. Even today, music students all over the world continue to study and perform his work. His operas and symphonies are still performed today.

1. Read this sentence from the passage.

   He has composed over 600 pieces of classical music.

   What does the word <u>composed</u> most likely refer to?
   - Ⓐ   Playing a song
   - Ⓑ   Writing a song
   - Ⓒ   Singing a song
   - Ⓓ   Listening to a song

2. What type of passage is "Mozart"?
   - Ⓐ   Realistic fiction
   - Ⓑ   Biography
   - Ⓒ   Autobiography
   - Ⓓ   Fable

3. If the passage were given another title, which title would best fit?
   - Ⓐ   The Life of a Great Composer
   - Ⓑ   How to Compose Music
   - Ⓒ   Living in Austria
   - Ⓓ   Learn the Piano Today

4 Mozart can be described as gifted. Give **two** details that show that Mozart was gifted.

1: _____

_____

2: _____

_____

5 Complete the chart below by describing **two** places that Mozart lived after Austria and what he did in each place.

Place	Details
Austria	Worked as a court musician

6 In what way can Mozart's life be considered sad? Use details from the passage to support your answer.

_____

_____

_____

_____

_____

Michelangelo

Born in 1475, Michelangelo was a genius of both academics and artistry. He lived during the Renaissance, which was a time in Europe when art was thriving. He was considered a typical Renaissance man. This term refers to people who have talents in many different areas. While he is best known as an artist and sculptor, he was also a poet, an engineer, and an architect.

Michelangelo's work became renowned pieces of the period in which he lived. The Statue of David, completed in 1504, is arguably one of Michelangelo's most famous works. It was sculpted from marble, and took over two years to complete.

A less known fact about the statue is that it was originally intended to be placed on the roof of the Florence Cathedral. Just before it was complete, people realized that placing it on the Florence Cathedral would be impossible. The statue weighed over 6 ton. While the roof would probably be able to support the weight, it would have been almost impossible to lift the statue to put it up there. This was in the 1500s before cranes and other machinery would have made the task a lot simpler! The statue was placed in a public square in Florence instead. It can be found today at the Academy of Fine Arts in Florence. Visitors to Florence can also see a replica of the famous statue where it was originally placed.

A close-up view of The Statue of David shows the striking detail of the sculpture.

7   What does the close-up view of The Statue of David best help readers understand?

   Ⓐ   Why the statue was so heavy

   Ⓑ   Why the statue lasted so long

   Ⓒ   Why the statue took so long to complete

   Ⓓ   Why the statue was placed in a public square

8   In the first paragraph, the word <u>thriving</u> shows that art was —

   Ⓐ   costly

   Ⓑ   varied

   Ⓒ   disliked

   Ⓓ   popular

9   Which sentence best supports the idea that Michelangelo was a "typical Renaissance man"?

   Ⓐ   *This term refers to people who have talents in many different areas.*

   Ⓑ   *While he is best known as an artist and sculptor, he was also a poet, an engineer, and an architect.*

   Ⓒ   *Michelangelo's work became renowned pieces of the period in which he lived.*

   Ⓓ   *The Statue of David, completed in 1504, is arguably one of Michelangelo's most famous works.*

10 Why wasn't the statue placed on the roof of the Florence Cathedral? Use details from the passage to support your answer.

___

11 The passage describes how The Statue of David took over two years to complete. What does this detail suggest about Michelangelo and his work?

___

12 Think about what you learned about Mozart and Michelangelo. Describe at least **one** way they are similar and at least **one** way they are different. Use details from both passages in your answer.

END OF SET 14

ANSWER KEY

Common Core State Standards

Student learning and assessment is based on the skills listed in the Massachusetts Curriculum Framework. This framework has the same content as the Common Core State Standards, except that a few additional skills are included. Just like the real PARCC assessments, the questions in this book test whether students have the knowledge and skills described in the Common Core State Standards. The English Language Arts standards assessed include both reading and writing standards.

Common Core Reading Standards

The majority of the questions assess reading standards. These standards are divided into two areas: Reading Standards for Literature and Reading Standards for Informational Text. The answer key on the following pages lists the main standard assessed by each question.

Common Core Writing Standards

Writing standards are also assessed on the PARCC tests. The last questions in the Literary Analysis Tasks and Research Simulation Tasks are essay questions. These questions assess a reading standard as well as one of the writing standards below.

- Write opinion pieces on topics or texts, supporting a point of view with reasons and information.
- Write informative/explanatory texts to examine a topic and convey ideas and information clearly.

The last question in the Narrative Writing Task assesses only writing standards. The main standard assessed is given below.

- Write narratives to develop real or imagined experiences or events using effective technique, descriptive details, and clear event sequences.

As well as covering the major standards listed above, these questions also cover other more general writing and language standards.

Scoring Questions

The answer key gives guidance on how to score technology-enhanced, constructed-response, essay, and narrative writing questions. Use the criteria listed as a guide to scoring these questions, and as a guide for giving the student advice on how to improve an answer.

PARCC Practice, Set 1, Literary Analysis Task

Question	Answer	Common Core Reading Standard for Literature
1	C	Determine the meaning of words and phrases as they are used in a text, including those that allude to significant characters found in mythology (e.g., Herculean).
2	B	Determine the meaning of words and phrases as they are used in a text, including those that allude to significant characters found in mythology (e.g., Herculean).
3	B	Determine a theme of a story, drama, or poem from details in the text; summarize the text.
4	D	Explain major differences between poems, drama, and prose, and refer to the structural elements of poems and drama when writing or speaking about a text.
5	B	Refer to details and examples in a text when explaining what the text says explicitly and when drawing inferences from the text.
6	B	Determine a theme of a story, drama, or poem from details in the text; summarize the text.
7	old wise	Describe in depth a character, setting, or event in a story or drama, drawing on specific details in the text (e.g., a character's thoughts, words, or actions).
8	See Below	Describe in depth a character, setting, or event in a story or drama, drawing on specific details in the text (e.g., a character's thoughts, words, or actions).
9	B	Refer to details and examples in a text when explaining what the text says explicitly and when drawing inferences from the text.
10	See Below	Compare and contrast the point of view from which different stories are narrated, including the difference between first- and third-person narrations.
11	See Below	Describe in depth a character, setting, or event in a story or drama, drawing on specific details in the text (e.g., a character's thoughts, words, or actions).
12	See Below	Make connections between the text of a story or drama and a visual or oral presentation of the text, identifying where each version reflects specific descriptions and directions in the text.
13	C	Determine the meaning of words and phrases as they are used in a text, including those that allude to significant characters found in mythology (e.g., Herculean).
14	B	Determine the meaning of words and phrases as they are used in a text, including those that allude to significant characters found in mythology (e.g., Herculean).
15	C	Refer to details and examples in a text when explaining what the text says explicitly and when drawing inferences from the text.
16	See Below	Describe in depth a character, setting, or event in a story or drama, drawing on specific details in the text (e.g., a character's thoughts, words, or actions).
17	C	Refer to details and examples in a text when explaining what the text says explicitly and when drawing inferences from the text.
18	B	Determine a theme of a story, drama, or poem from details in the text; summarize the text.
19	A	Determine a theme of a story, drama, or poem from details in the text; summarize the text.
20	See Below	Describe in depth a character, setting, or event in a story or drama, drawing on specific details in the text (e.g., a character's thoughts, words, or actions).
21	See Below	Describe in depth a character, setting, or event in a story or drama, drawing on specific details in the text (e.g., a character's thoughts, words, or actions).
22	See Below	Determine the meaning of words and phrases as they are used in a text, including those that allude to significant characters found in mythology (e.g., Herculean).
23	See Below	Refer to details and examples in a text when explaining what the text says explicitly and when drawing inferences from the text.
24	See Below	Compare and contrast the treatment of similar themes and topics and patterns of events in stories, myths, and traditional literature from different cultures.

Q8.
Give a score of 0, 1, or 2 based on how well the answer meets the criteria listed below.
- It should describe how Chloe removes the gray hairs because she doesn't want him to look old.
- It should describe how the mother removes the darker hairs because she wants him to look gray and wise.

Q10.
Give a score of 0, 1, or 2 based on how well the answer meets the criteria listed below.
- It should make a reasonable inference about how Arnold feels at the end of the passage based on the events.
- It may infer that Arnold is pleased that he is not stuck in the middle or happy that everyone is going to get along.

Q11.
Give a score of 1 for each cause box correctly completed.
- The box for Chloe's actions should refer to how she plucks out his gray hairs.
- The box for the mother's actions should refer to how she plucks out his darker hairs.

Q12.
Give a score of 0, 1, or 2 based on how well the answer meets the criteria listed below.
- It should explain that the art shows how Arnold changes over time or how he loses his hair.
- It should use relevant details from the passage.

Q16.
Give a score of 0, 1, or 2 based on how many relevant details are given.
- Any detail from the passage that shows Simon's kindness can be accepted.
- The student may describe how he thanks his mother for the games, how he does not argue with Thomas, how he tries to say that Thomas can play his games, or how he quickly agrees to share the games.

Q20.
Give a score of 0, 1, or 2 based on how well the answer meets the criteria listed below.
- The student should circle one of the words and provide an explanation to support the choice.
- Either answer is acceptable as long as the student explains it and supports it with relevant details.

Q21.
Give a score of 0, 1, or 2 based on how well the answer meets the criteria listed below.
- It should give an explanation that refers to how Thomas realizes he cannot use his system without Simon's games.
- It should identify that the decision is still selfish because Thomas only shares because it benefits him.

Q22.
Give a score of 0, 1, or 2 based on how well the answer meets the criteria listed below.
- The student should show an understanding that the phrase shows Thomas's feelings or emotions.
- It should explain that the phrase "his eyes lit up" shows Thomas's interest, excitement, or happiness.

Q23.
Give a score of 0, 1, or 2 based on how well the answer meets the criteria listed below.
- The student should select and circle three words that show that Thomas feels grumpy. The possible words could include *frown*, *gruffly*, *whined*, *shrugged*, or *firmly*.
- It should include a reasonable explanation that relates the words to how Thomas feels.

Q24.
Give a total score out of 10 as described below.
- Give a score of 0, 1, 2, or 3 based on how well the answer shows an understanding of the passages and uses relevant details from both passages.
- Give a score of 0, 1, 2, or 3 based on how well the student expresses ideas. The answer should be well-developed, focused, well-organized, have good transitions, and have an introduction and a conclusion.
- Give a score of 0, 1, 2, 3, or 4 based on how well the student uses the conventions of standard English. The answer should be well-written and have few or no errors in spelling, grammar, punctuation, or capitalization.

PARCC Practice, Set 2, Research Simulation Task

Question	Answer	Common Core Reading Standard for Informational Text
1	D	Determine the meaning of general academic and domain-specific words or phrases in a text relevant to a grade 4 topic or subject area.
2	again	Determine the meaning of general academic and domain-specific words or phrases in a text relevant to a grade 4 topic or subject area.
3	A	Refer to details and examples in a text when explaining what the text says explicitly and when drawing inferences from the text.
4	A	Compare and contrast a firsthand and secondhand account of the same event or topic; describe the differences in focus and the information provided.
5	B	Determine the main idea of a text and explain how it is supported by key details; summarize the text.
6	3rd, 4th, & 6th	Compare and contrast a firsthand and secondhand account of the same event or topic; describe the differences in focus and the information provided.
7	A	Explain how an author uses reasons and evidence to support particular points in a text.
8	B	Describe the overall structure (e.g., chronology, comparison, cause/effect, problem/solution) of events, ideas, concepts, or information in a text or part of a text.
9	See Below	Explain events, procedures, ideas, or concepts in a historical, scientific, or technical text, including what happened and why, based on specific information in the text.
10	C	Determine the meaning of general academic and domain-specific words or phrases in a text relevant to a grade 4 topic or subject area.
11	B	Determine the meaning of general academic and domain-specific words or phrases in a text relevant to a grade 4 topic or subject area.
12	1860	Refer to details and examples in a text when explaining what the text says explicitly and when drawing inferences from the text.
13	C	Determine the main idea of a text and explain how it is supported by key details; summarize the text.
14	D	Compare and contrast a firsthand and secondhand account of the same event or topic; describe the differences in focus and the information provided.
15	C	Refer to details and examples in a text when explaining what the text says explicitly and when drawing inferences from the text.
16	See Below	Explain events, procedures, ideas, or concepts in a historical, scientific, or technical text, including what happened and why, based on specific information in the text.
17	See Below	Determine the main idea of a text and explain how it is supported by key details; summarize the text.
18	See Below	Refer to details and examples in a text when explaining what the text says explicitly and when drawing inferences from the text.
19	B	Determine the meaning of general academic and domain-specific words or phrases in a text relevant to a grade 4 topic or subject area.
20	A	Refer to details and examples in a text when explaining what the text says explicitly and when drawing inferences from the text.
21	B	Explain how an author uses reasons and evidence to support particular points in a text.
22	See Below	Determine the main idea of a text and explain how it is supported by key details; summarize the text.
23	See Below	Describe the overall structure (e.g., chronology, comparison, cause/effect, problem/solution) of events, ideas, concepts, or information in a text or part of a text.
24	See Below	Explain events, procedures, ideas, or concepts in a historical, scientific, or technical text, including what happened and why, based on specific information in the text.
25	See Below	Integrate information from two texts on the same topic in order to write or speak about the subject knowledgeably.

Q9.
Give a score of 0, 1, 2, or 3 based on how many correct actions are listed.
- The actions listed should be that he was stripped of his title, that he was arrested, and that he had his boxing license taken away.

Q16.
Give a score of 0, 1, or 2 based on how many correct actions are listed.
- The actions listed could include that he gave speeches, wrote letters, led the fight against the South in the Civil War, or issued an order that ended slavery.

Q17.
Give a score of 0, 1, or 2 based on how well the answer meets the criteria listed below.
- It should provide a clear and accurate description of two of Abraham Lincoln's achievements.
- The achievements identified could be becoming president, ending the civil war, helping to unite the nation, or helping to end slavery.

Q18.
Give a score of 0, 1, or 2 based on how well the answer meets the criteria listed below.
- The student should give a reasonable explanation of how Lincoln's background affects how he or she feels about his achievements.
- The answer may refer to admiring him more, respecting him more, or being more amazed by what he was able to achieve.

Q22.
Give a score of 0, 1, or 2 based on how well the answer meets the criteria listed below.
- It should explain that Amelia Earhart was a pioneer because she did things that no woman had ever done before.
- It may describe how she was the first woman to fly solo across the Atlantic Ocean, how she set many records, or how female pilots were rare at the time.

Q23.
Give a score of 0, 1, or 2 based on how well the answer meets the criteria listed below.
- It should explain that the second paragraph describes Amelia's disappearance.
- It may describe the second paragraph's purpose as being to describe a mystery surrounding Amelia Earhart.

Q24.
Give a score of 0, 1, or 2 based on how well the answer meets the criteria listed below.
- The student should infer that the events would not be as significant today and give a reasonable explanation to support the inference.
- Students may describe how flight has advanced, so flying across an ocean solo is no longer a remarkable achievement. Students may also describe how female pilots are not rare like they were at the time, so a woman flying a plane is not as significant or unusual.

Q25.
Give a total score out of 10 as described below.
- Give a score of 0, 1, 2, or 3 based on how well the answer uses relevant information from all three passages and synthesizes ideas from the passages.
- Give a score of 0, 1, 2, or 3 based on how well the student expresses ideas. The answer should be well-developed, focused, well-organized, and have a style that is appropriate to the task.
- Give a score of 0, 1, 2, 3, or 4 based on how well the student uses the conventions of standard English. The answer should be well-written and have few or no errors in spelling, grammar, punctuation, or capitalization.

PARCC Practice, Set 3, Narrative Writing Task

Question	Answer	Common Core Reading Standard for Literature
1	C	Determine the meaning of words and phrases as they are used in a text, including those that allude to significant characters found in mythology (e.g., Herculean).
2	B	Determine the meaning of words and phrases as they are used in a text, including those that allude to significant characters found in mythology (e.g., Herculean).
3	Maria	Explain major differences between poems, drama, and prose, and refer to the structural elements of poems and drama when writing or speaking about a text.
4	See Below	Explain major differences between poems, drama, and prose, and refer to the structural elements of poems and drama when writing or speaking about a text.
5	B	Determine the meaning of words and phrases as they are used in a text, including those that allude to significant characters found in mythology (e.g., Herculean).
6	C	Compare and contrast the point of view from which different stories are narrated, including the difference between first- and third-person narrations.
7	A	Describe in depth a character, setting, or event in a story or drama, drawing on specific details in the text (e.g., a character's thoughts, words, or actions).
8	2, 1, 4, 3	Describe in depth a character, setting, or event in a story or drama, drawing on specific details in the text (e.g., a character's thoughts, words, or actions).
9	D	Determine a theme of a story, drama, or poem from details in the text; summarize the text.
10	B	Determine a theme of a story, drama, or poem from details in the text; summarize the text.
11	See Below	Refer to details and examples in a text when explaining what the text says explicitly and when drawing inferences from the text.
12	See Below	This question assesses the writing standard below. Write narratives to develop real or imagined experiences or events using effective technique, descriptive details, and clear event sequences.

Q4.
Give a score of 0, 1, or 2 based on how many reasonable features are given.
- The student may describe how the passage introduces Maria in the first sentence, how the passage opens by describing Maria's feelings, how the passage mainly describes Maria, how the passage is focused on Maria's problem, or how the passage tells how Maria changes.

Q11.
Give a score of 0, 1, or 2 based on how well the answer meets the criteria listed below.
- It should provide a reasonable analysis of how Maria feels at the end of the story.
- It may refer to how she slumps in her chair and sighs as showing she is annoyed, fed up, or upset.
- It should explain that she feels that way because of how she changed to look like Sarah only to find that Sarah changed to look like her.

Q12.
Give a total score out of 7 as described below.
- Give a score of 0, 1, 2, or 3 based on the student's narrative writing skill. The narrative should establish a situation, have a clear event sequence, use effective descriptions, use concrete words and phrases and sensory details, and provide a sense of closure.
- Give a score of 0, 1, 2, 3, or 4 based on how well the student uses the conventions of standard English. The answer should be well-written and have few or no errors in spelling, grammar, punctuation, or capitalization.

PARCC Practice, Set 4, Short Informational Text

Question	Answer	Common Core Reading Standard for Informational Text
1	A	Determine the meaning of general academic and domain-specific words or phrases in a text relevant to a grade 4 topic or subject area.
2	C	Interpret information presented visually, orally, or quantitatively and explain how the information contributes to an understanding of the text in which it appears.
3	See Below	Interpret information presented visually, orally, or quantitatively and explain how the information contributes to an understanding of the text in which it appears.
4	F, F, F, O, F, O, F	Compare and contrast a firsthand and secondhand account of the same event or topic; describe the differences in focus and the information provided.
5	C	Describe the overall structure (e.g., chronology, comparison, cause/effect, problem/solution) of events, ideas, concepts, or information in a text or part of a text.
6	B	Determine the main idea of a text and explain how it is supported by key details; summarize the text.
7	D	Refer to details and examples in a text when explaining what the text says explicitly and when drawing inferences from the text.
8	See Below	Refer to details and examples in a text when explaining what the text says explicitly and when drawing inferences from the text.
9	D	Compare and contrast a firsthand and secondhand account of the same event or topic; describe the differences in focus and the information provided.
10	See Below	Explain how an author uses reasons and evidence to support particular points in a text.
11	See Below	Explain events, procedures, ideas, or concepts in a historical, scientific, or technical text, including what happened and why, based on specific information in the text.
12	See Below	Determine the main idea of a text and explain how it is supported by key details; summarize the text.

Q3.
Give a score of 0, 1, or 2 based on how many examples are given of things that can be inferred from the table.
- The student may refer to how De Niro has been making movies constantly since 1973, how the number of movies is greatest in the 1990s, how he is still making movies in recent times, or how only a few of the movies are comedies.

Q8.
Give a score of 0, 1, or 2 based on how many correct supporting details are given.
- The supporting details given should be those that show either De Niro's or Scorsese's success.
- The answer may refer to their Academy Award wins, how they both received the Cecil B. DeMille Award, or how the films they worked on together won awards. The answer may also refer to details that show just De Niro's success.

Q10.
Give a score of 0, 1, or 2 based on how many correct supporting details are given.
- Possible answers include that De Niro won an Academy Award for *Mean Streets*, that De Niro won an Academy Award for *Raging Bull*, or that they worked together on several box office hits.

Q11.
Give a score of 0, 1, or 2 based on how well the answer meets the criteria listed below.
- It should analyze how the sentence helps show the significance of De Niro receiving the award.
- It should explain how it suggests that only great actors receive the award or how it shows what the award means.

Q12.
Give a score of 0, 1, 2, or 3 based on how well the answer meets the criteria listed below.
- It should provide a reasonable analysis of how the author shows Robert De Niro's success.
- The answer may refer to awards he was won, the great films he has been in, the number or range of films he has been in, or statements made such as him being "one of the finest actors of his time."

PARCC Practice, Set 5, Short Literary Text

Question	Answer	Common Core Reading Standard for Literature
1	B	Determine the meaning of words and phrases as they are used in a text, including those that allude to significant characters found in mythology (e.g., Herculean).
2	D	Determine the meaning of words and phrases as they are used in a text, including those that allude to significant characters found in mythology (e.g., Herculean).
3	A	Determine a theme of a story, drama, or poem from details in the text; summarize the text.
4	A	Determine the meaning of words and phrases as they are used in a text, including those that allude to significant characters found in mythology (e.g., Herculean).
5	A	Refer to details and examples in a text when explaining what the text says explicitly and when drawing inferences from the text.
6	upset understanding	Describe in depth a character, setting, or event in a story or drama, drawing on specific details in the text (e.g., a character's thoughts, words, or actions).
7	See Below	Describe in depth a character, setting, or event in a story or drama, drawing on specific details in the text (e.g., a character's thoughts, words, or actions).
8	B	Compare and contrast the point of view from which different stories are narrated, including the difference between first- and third-person narrations.
9	A	Refer to details and examples in a text when explaining what the text says explicitly and when drawing inferences from the text.
10	See Below	Describe in depth a character, setting, or event in a story or drama, drawing on specific details in the text (e.g., a character's thoughts, words, or actions).
11	See Below	Refer to details and examples in a text when explaining what the text says explicitly and when drawing inferences from the text.
12	See Below	Determine a theme of a story, drama, or poem from details in the text; summarize the text.

Q7.
Give a score of 1 for each correct sentence circled that includes a reasonable explanation.
- Any sentence from the fifth sentence onward can be accepted.
- Each explanation should describe what the sentence shows about how Rory feels and indicate that he feels either upset or understanding.

Q10.
Give a score of 0, 1, or 2 based on how well the answer meets the criteria listed below.
- It should state whether the student believes that Rory admires his sister.
- It should provide a fully-supported explanation of why the student has this opinion.
- It should use relevant details from the passage.

Q11.
Give a score of 0, 1, 2, or 3 based on how many rows of the table are correctly completed.
- Rory should be described as completing his exams.
- Rory's mother should be described as trying to get fit.
- Rory's father should be described as working hard at his new job.

Q12.
Give a score of 0, 1, 2, or 3 based on how well the answer meets the criteria listed below.
- It should give a reasonable example of how Rory is motivated by his sister.
- It should refer to how Rory is motivated by his sister's hard work and also hopes to attend college.
- It should use at least three details from the passage.

PARCC Practice, Set 6, Long Informational Text

Question	Answer	Common Core Reading Standard for Informational Text
1	A	Refer to details and examples in a text when explaining what the text says explicitly and when drawing inferences from the text.
2	See Below	Determine the meaning of general academic and domain-specific words or phrases in a text relevant to a grade 4 topic or subject area.
3	B	Interpret information presented visually, orally, or quantitatively and explain how the information contributes to an understanding of the text in which it appears.
4	B	Explain events, procedures, ideas, or concepts in a historical, scientific, or technical text, including what happened and why, based on specific information in the text.
5	A	Refer to details and examples in a text when explaining what the text says explicitly and when drawing inferences from the text.
6	A	Compare and contrast a firsthand and secondhand account of the same event or topic; describe the differences in focus and the information provided.
7	C	Describe the overall structure (e.g., chronology, comparison, cause/effect, problem/solution) of events, ideas, concepts, or information in a text or part of a text.
8	See Below	Interpret information presented visually, orally, or quantitatively and explain how the information contributes to an understanding of the text in which it appears.
9	C	Interpret information presented visually, orally, or quantitatively and explain how the information contributes to an understanding of the text in which it appears.
10	See Below	Determine the main idea of a text and explain how it is supported by key details; summarize the text.
11	See Below	Explain events, procedures, ideas, or concepts in a historical, scientific, or technical text, including what happened and why, based on specific information in the text.
12	See Below	Explain how an author uses reasons and evidence to support particular points in a text.

Q2.
Give a score of 0, 1, or 2 based on how well the answer meets the criteria listed below.
- It should explain the effect of the word *lush* and describe how it helps create an image of the desert.
- It should show an understanding of the dictionary meaning of the word, as well as the connotation.
- Students may describe how it makes the savannah seem green, thriving, fertile, or pleasant.

Q8.
Give a score of 0.5 for each correct country listed.
- Possible answers include Morocco, Tunisia, Algeria, Libya, Egypt, Mauritania, Mali, Niger, Chad, and Sudan.

Q10.
Give a score of 0, 1, or 2 based on how well the answer meets the criteria listed below.
- It should state a prediction of whether or not the Sahara Desert will stay the same in the future.
- It may include an explanation related to how the desert has changed in the past, or it may provide an explanation related to the current developments described in the last paragraph.

Q11.
Give a score of 1 for each interesting or surprising detail given that includes a reasonable explanation.
- Any reasonable details can be accepted as long as the choice is explained.
- The student could refer to how animals once lived in the desert, to how large the desert is, to how the desert has changed, to how it sometimes snows, or to how there are plans to build a road across it.

Q12.
Give a score of 0, 1, 2, or 3 based on how well the answer meets the criteria listed below.
- It should describe at least three things that would make life in the Sahara Desert difficult.
- The student may refer to the large distances, the sand dunes, the lack of roads, or the dry climate.
- It should use relevant details from the passage.

PARCC Practice, Set 7, Paired Literary Passages

Question	Answer	Common Core Reading Standard for Literature
1	B	Refer to details and examples in a text when explaining what the text says explicitly and when drawing inferences from the text.
2	D	Compare and contrast the point of view from which different stories are narrated, including the difference between first- and third-person narrations.
3	A	Describe in depth a character, setting, or event in a story or drama, drawing on specific details in the text (e.g., a character's thoughts, words, or actions).
4	C	Make connections between the text of a story or drama and a visual or oral presentation of the text, identifying where each version reflects specific descriptions and directions in the text.
5	See Below	Explain major differences between poems, drama, and prose, and refer to the structural elements of poems and drama when writing or speaking about a text.
6	See Below	Determine a theme of a story, drama, or poem from details in the text; summarize the text.
7	B	Determine the meaning of words and phrases as they are used in a text, including those that allude to significant characters found in mythology (e.g., Herculean).
8	C	Determine a theme of a story, drama, or poem from details in the text; summarize the text.
9	A	Refer to details and examples in a text when explaining what the text says explicitly and when drawing inferences from the text.
10	See Below	Describe in depth a character, setting, or event in a story or drama, drawing on specific details in the text (e.g., a character's thoughts, words, or actions).
11	See Below	Explain major differences between poems, drama, and prose, and refer to the structural elements of poems and drama when writing or speaking about a text.
12	See Below	Compare and contrast the treatment of similar themes and topics and patterns of events in stories, myths, and traditional literature from different cultures.

Q5.
Give a score of 0, 1, or 2 based on how well the answer meets the criteria listed below.
- It should identify that the passage is meant to be humorous and explain how you can tell.
- The analysis may refer to the characters, the plot, or the tone.

Q6.
Give a score of 0.5 for each step in the summary that explains what happens to result in the bag of cannolis being empty.
- A sample of the missing steps is as follows: ... → Tony gives Vinnie a few cannolis. → Tony gives Jen a handful of cannolis. → Tony gives Mr. Jackson a cannoli. → Tony gives Uncle Benny the bag. → ...

Q10.
Give a score of 0, 1, or 2 based on how well the answer meets the criteria listed below.
- It should describe how Max feels upset, annoyed, or determined at the start of the passage.
- It should describe how Max feels relieved, embarrassed, or amused at the end of the passage.

Q11.
Give a score of 0, 1, or 2 based on how well the answer meets the criteria listed below.
- It should describe how the author creates a sense of panic and include at least three words or phrases used.
- It may refer to Max's actions in the first paragraph, such as "flipping wildly" through pages and "pinning up hastily written notes." It may also refer to specific words used like *paced*, *stared*, and *scribbled*.

Q12.
Give a score of 0, 1, 2, or 3 based on how well the answer meets the criteria listed below.
- It should compare the mistake made by Tony and Max in the passages. It should identify that Tony does not realize he gave Uncle Benny an empty bag, while Max does realize that he ate the cookies and then forgot about it.
- It should provide a reasonable analysis of how this affects how each passage ends.

PARCC Practice, Set 8, Literary Analysis Task

Question	Answer	Common Core Reading Standard for Literature
1	C	Determine the meaning of words and phrases as they are used in a text, including those that allude to significant characters found in mythology (e.g., Herculean).
2	A	Make connections between the text of a story or drama and a visual or oral presentation of the text, identifying where each version reflects specific descriptions and directions in the text.
3	3, 2, 1, 4	Describe in depth a character, setting, or event in a story or drama, drawing on specific details in the text (e.g., a character's thoughts, words, or actions).
4	B	Determine the meaning of words and phrases as they are used in a text, including those that allude to significant characters found in mythology (e.g., Herculean).
5	gulped gripped trembling	Refer to details and examples in a text when explaining what the text says explicitly and when drawing inferences from the text.
6	See Below	Describe in depth a character, setting, or event in a story or drama, drawing on specific details in the text (e.g., a character's thoughts, words, or actions).
7	B	Refer to details and examples in a text when explaining what the text says explicitly and when drawing inferences from the text.
8	D	Determine the meaning of words and phrases as they are used in a text, including those that allude to significant characters found in mythology (e.g., Herculean).
9	See Below	Describe in depth a character, setting, or event in a story or drama, drawing on specific details in the text (e.g., a character's thoughts, words, or actions).
10	See Below	Explain major differences between poems, drama, and prose, and refer to the structural elements of poems and drama when writing or speaking about a text.
11	See Below	Describe in depth a character, setting, or event in a story or drama, drawing on specific details in the text (e.g., a character's thoughts, words, or actions).
12	See Below	Refer to details and examples in a text when explaining what the text says explicitly and when drawing inferences from the text.
13	B	Determine a theme of a story, drama, or poem from details in the text; summarize the text.
14	See Below	Determine a theme of a story, drama, or poem from details in the text; summarize the text.
15	C	Describe in depth a character, setting, or event in a story or drama, drawing on specific details in the text (e.g., a character's thoughts, words, or actions).
16	pranks, tricks	Determine the meaning of words and phrases as they are used in a text, including those that allude to significant characters found in mythology (e.g., Herculean).
17	A	Refer to details and examples in a text when explaining what the text says explicitly and when drawing inferences from the text.
18	B	Explain major differences between poems, drama, and prose, and refer to the structural elements of poems and drama when writing or speaking about a text.
19	C	Refer to details and examples in a text when explaining what the text says explicitly and when drawing inferences from the text.
20	See Below	Describe in depth a character, setting, or event in a story or drama, drawing on specific details in the text (e.g., a character's thoughts, words, or actions).
21	D	Explain major differences between poems, drama, and prose, and refer to the structural elements of poems and drama when writing or speaking about a text.
22	See Below	Describe in depth a character, setting, or event in a story or drama, drawing on specific details in the text (e.g., a character's thoughts, words, or actions).
23	See Below	Refer to details and examples in a text when explaining what the text says explicitly and when drawing inferences from the text.
24	See Below	Compare and contrast the treatment of similar themes and topics and patterns of events in stories, myths, and traditional literature from different cultures.

Q6.
Give a score of 0, 1, or 2 based on how well the answer meets the criteria listed below.
- It should describe how Steven suggests the trick, hides in the closet, and then leaps out.
- It should describe how Jason pretends to sleep and then suggests checking the closet.

Q9.
Give a score of 0, 1, or 2 based on how well the answer meets the criteria listed below.
- It should give a reasonable explanation of why Jason has to stop himself from smiling.
- It should show an understanding that Jason knows what the noise is and knows what is about to happen.

Q10.
Give a score of 0.5 for each sentence circled that helps create suspense. Give a score of 0, 1, or 2 for the explanation.
- The student should explain why the two sentences were chosen and describe how they help create suspense.

Q11.
Give a score of 0, 1, or 2 based on how well the answer meets the criteria listed below.
- It should state an opinion of whether the trick was mean or funny.
- It should use relevant details from the passage to support the opinion.

Q12.
Give a score of 0, 1, or 2 based on how many reasonable details are given to support the idea that Marvin found the trick either mean or funny. The student may circle either sentence, and will be scored on how the sentence chosen is supported.
- To support the idea that the trick was mean, the student may describe how Marvin is scared by the trick, how he shrieks and falls backwards, how Steven and Jason laugh at him, or how he sleeps with the lamp on.
- To support the idea that the trick was funny, the student may describe how Marvin laughs about the trick, how he tries to be annoyed but can't, how he doesn't seem mad about it, or how he says "nice one guys."

Q14.
Give a score of 0, 1, or 2 based on how well the answer meets the criteria listed below.
- It should give a reasonable explanation of why the student chose the title.
- It should relate the title to the theme or the plot of the passage.

Q20.
Give a score of 0, 1, 2, or 3 based on how many correct details are listed in the diagram.
- Possible details include that he stood completely still, that he did not want to turn around, that he stared straight ahead, that he thought about running to his tent, or that he leapt when his father touched him.

Q22.
Give a score of 0, 1, or 2 based on how many plausible reasons are given.
- The reasons could include that she was tired of him playing tricks on her, that she wanted to get him back, that she hoped he would stop playing tricks, that her father suggested it, or that she thought it would be fun.

Q23.
Give a score of 0, 1, or 2 based on how well the answer meets the criteria listed below.
- It should state whether or not Lucas will stop playing tricks on Molly in the future and explain the answer.
- The student may infer that Lucas now knows what it is like to be scared and so will stop, or that he will play more tricks to get her back.

Q24.
Give a total score out of 10 as described below.
- Give a score of 0, 1, 2, or 3 based on how well the answer shows an understanding of the passages and uses relevant details from both passages.
- Give a score of 0, 1, 2, or 3 based on how well the student expresses ideas. The answer should be well-developed, focused, well-organized, have good transitions, and have an introduction and a conclusion.
- Give a score of 0, 1, 2, 3, or 4 based on how well the student uses the conventions of standard English. The answer should be well-written and have few or no errors in spelling, grammar, punctuation, or capitalization.

PARCC Practice, Set 9, Research Simulation Task

Question	Answer	Common Core Reading Standard for Informational Text
1	B	Determine the meaning of general academic and domain-specific words or phrases in a text relevant to a grade 4 topic or subject area.
2	B	Refer to details and examples in a text when explaining what the text says explicitly and when drawing inferences from the text.
3	C	Compare and contrast a firsthand and secondhand account of the same event or topic; describe the differences in focus and the information provided.
4	A	Compare and contrast a firsthand and secondhand account of the same event or topic; describe the differences in focus and the information provided.
5	See Below	Compare and contrast a firsthand and secondhand account of the same event or topic; describe the differences in focus and the information provided.
6	Communication Teamwork	Refer to details and examples in a text when explaining what the text says explicitly and when drawing inferences from the text.
7	A	Determine the main idea of a text and explain how it is supported by key details; summarize the text.
8	D	Compare and contrast a firsthand and secondhand account of the same event or topic; describe the differences in focus and the information provided.
9	4th and 5th	Explain how an author uses reasons and evidence to support particular points in a text.
10	C	Determine the meaning of general academic and domain-specific words or phrases in a text relevant to a grade 4 topic or subject area.
11	A	Determine the meaning of general academic and domain-specific words or phrases in a text relevant to a grade 4 topic or subject area.
12	A	Describe the overall structure (e.g., chronology, comparison, cause/effect, problem/solution) of events, ideas, concepts, or information in a text or part of a text.
13	See Below	Explain how an author uses reasons and evidence to support particular points in a text.
14	See Below	Refer to details and examples in a text when explaining what the text says explicitly and when drawing inferences from the text.
15	D	Interpret information presented visually, orally, or quantitatively and explain how the information contributes to an understanding of the text in which it appears.
16	C	Determine the main idea of a text and explain how it is supported by key details; summarize the text.
17	D	Refer to details and examples in a text when explaining what the text says explicitly and when drawing inferences from the text.
18	See Below	Determine the main idea of a text and explain how it is supported by key details; summarize the text.
19	See Below	Compare and contrast a firsthand and secondhand account of the same event or topic; describe the differences in focus and the information provided.
20	See Below	Refer to details and examples in a text when explaining what the text says explicitly and when drawing inferences from the text.
21	D	Describe the overall structure (e.g., chronology, comparison, cause/effect, problem/solution) of events, ideas, concepts, or information in a text or part of a text.
22	C	Determine the meaning of general academic and domain-specific words or phrases in a text relevant to a grade 4 topic or subject area.
23	C	Interpret information presented visually, orally, or quantitatively and explain how the information contributes to an understanding of the text in which it appears.
24	See Below	Explain how an author uses reasons and evidence to support particular points in a text.
25	See Below	Integrate information from two texts on the same topic in order to write or speak about the subject knowledgeably.

Q5.
Give a score of 1 for each paragraph selected that includes a reasonable explanation of how it shows who the main audience is.
- Any of the paragraphs could reasonably be selected, but the selections made must be explained.
- The explanation should describe who the paragraph is addressed to or who the information in the paragraph is designed to appeal to.

Q13.
Give a score of 0, 1, or 2 based on how well the answer meets the criteria listed below.
- It should explain how the camp encourages children to take part in sports and other activities.
- It may refer to how there are many sports and activities on offer, how children can run around, how children can try new activities, how there are fitness classes, or how the fitness program will be enjoyable.

Q14.
Give a score of 0.5 for each correct sport listed.
- Possible answers are football, soccer, baseball, basketball, athletics, tennis, rowing, or sailing.

Q18.
Give a score of 0, 1, or 2 based on how many correct benefits are given.
- The benefits may include that children get fit, that children become healthier, that children start liking sports, that children have fun, that children start to appreciate being active, or that children develop good fitness habits.

Q19.
Give a score of 0, 1, or 2 based on how well the answer meets the criteria listed below.
- It should explain that the information is biased toward making the camp sound good.
- The answer should show an understanding that the information is an advertisement or brochure, and is designed to make people want to attend the camp.

Q20.
Give a score of 1 for each group added to the table correctly. The correct groups are listed below.
- Cub Scouts, 7 to 11; Scouts, 11 to 18; Rover Scouts, over 18

Q24.
Give a score of 0, 1, or 2 based on how well the answer meets the criteria listed below.
- It should describe at least two ways the author tries to get young readers interested in becoming a scout.
- The student may refer to the examples of activities given, the way questions are asked, the positive examples given such as being "a swimmer that fears no waters," or the positive qualities mentioned.
- The student should also give an opinion on whether the author is successful.

Q25.
Give a total score out of 10 as described below.
- Give a score of 0, 1, 2, or 3 based on how well the answer uses relevant information from all three passages and synthesizes ideas from the passages.
- Give a score of 0, 1, 2, or 3 based on how well the student expresses ideas. The answer should be well-developed, focused, well-organized, and have a style that is appropriate to the task.
- Give a score of 0, 1, 2, 3, or 4 based on how well the student uses the conventions of standard English. The answer should be well-written and have few or no errors in spelling, grammar, punctuation, or capitalization.

PARCC Practice, Set 10, Narrative Writing Task

Question	Answer	Common Core Reading Standard for Literature
1	B	Determine the meaning of words and phrases as they are used in a text, including those that allude to significant characters found in mythology (e.g., Herculean).
2	B	Describe in depth a character, setting, or event in a story or drama, drawing on specific details in the text (e.g., a character's thoughts, words, or actions).
3	A	Explain major differences between poems, drama, and prose, and refer to the structural elements of poems and drama when writing or speaking about a text.
4	5th	Determine the meaning of words and phrases as they are used in a text, including those that allude to significant characters found in mythology (e.g., Herculean).
5	See Below	Make connections between the text of a story or drama and a visual or oral presentation of the text, identifying where each version reflects specific descriptions and directions in the text.
6	C	Explain major differences between poems, drama, and prose, and refer to the structural elements of poems and drama when writing or speaking about a text.
7	C	Describe in depth a character, setting, or event in a story or drama, drawing on specific details in the text (e.g., a character's thoughts, words, or actions).
8	C	Determine the meaning of words and phrases as they are used in a text, including those that allude to significant characters found in mythology (e.g., Herculean).
9	B	Refer to details and examples in a text when explaining what the text says explicitly and when drawing inferences from the text.
10	B	Make connections between the text of a story or drama and a visual or oral presentation of the text, identifying where each version reflects specific descriptions and directions in the text.
11	6	Explain major differences between poems, drama, and prose, and refer to the structural elements of poems and drama when writing or speaking about a text.
12	B	Describe in depth a character, setting, or event in a story or drama, drawing on specific details in the text (e.g., a character's thoughts, words, or actions).
13	See Below	Refer to details and examples in a text when explaining what the text says explicitly and when drawing inferences from the text.
14	See Below	This question assesses the writing standard below. Write narratives to develop real or imagined experiences or events using effective technique, descriptive details, and clear event sequences.

Q5.
Give a score of 0, 1, or 2 based on how well the answer meets the criteria listed below.
- It should give a reasonable explanation of the meaning of the simile.
- It should refer to how the simile compares the lion's mane to sunshine, which helps you imagine it being bright, radiant, or beautiful.

Q13.
Give a score of 0.5 for each correct word or phrase added to the table. Possible answers are listed below.
- Words to Show the Lion is Feared: fearful roar, scared all, run and hide, pray for their tomorrow, lair, truly frightening place.
- Words to Show the Lion is Harmless: roar became a whisper, soft sound, kindly home, hold his loved ones, met no harm, harmony, shared, tamed within an instant, gentle hand of love, calm forever.

Q14.
Give a total score out of 7 as described below.
- Give a score of 0, 1, 2, or 3 based on the student's narrative writing skill. The narrative should establish a situation, have a clear event sequence, use effective descriptions, use concrete words and phrases and sensory details, and provide a sense of closure.
- Give a score of 0, 1, 2, 3, or 4 based on how well the student uses the conventions of standard English. The answer should be well-written and have few or no errors in spelling, grammar, punctuation, or capitalization.

PARCC Practice, Set 11, Short Informational Text

Question	Answer	Common Core Reading Standard for Informational Text
1	C	Determine the meaning of general academic and domain-specific words or phrases in a text relevant to a grade 4 topic or subject area.
2	B	Determine the meaning of general academic and domain-specific words or phrases in a text relevant to a grade 4 topic or subject area.
3	Step 3, Step 6	Explain events, procedures, ideas, or concepts in a historical, scientific, or technical text, including what happened and why, based on specific information in the text.
4	See Below	Explain how an author uses reasons and evidence to support particular points in a text.
5	1st, 2nd, 5th	Refer to details and examples in a text when explaining what the text says explicitly and when drawing inferences from the text.
6	A	Determine the main idea of a text and explain how it is supported by key details; summarize the text.
7	C	Describe the overall structure (e.g., chronology, comparison, cause/effect, problem/solution) of events, ideas, concepts, or information in a text or part of a text.
8	See Below	Refer to details and examples in a text when explaining what the text says explicitly and when drawing inferences from the text.
9	C	Interpret information presented visually, orally, or quantitatively and explain how the information contributes to an understanding of the text in which it appears.
10	B	Explain events, procedures, ideas, or concepts in a historical, scientific, or technical text, including what happened and why, based on specific information in the text.
11	See Below	Refer to details and examples in a text when explaining what the text says explicitly and when drawing inferences from the text.
12	See Below	Explain events, procedures, ideas, or concepts in a historical, scientific, or technical text, including what happened and why, based on specific information in the text.

Q4.
Give a score of 0, 1, or 2 based on how many correct reasons are given.
- Possible reasons include that there may be knots and tangles, that you may hurt the dog if you comb too fast, that you may scare the dog if you comb too fast, or that you need to remove knots, tangles, or matted hair gently.

Q8.
Give a score of 0, 1, or 2 based on how well the answer meets the criteria listed below.
- It should provide a reasonable explanation of why the dog should be clean.
- It should include two problems that may occur if the dog is not clean.
- The answer may refer to the dog being hard to comb if it is dirty, to the dirt causing knots or tangles, or to the dirt causing the fur to pull. The student may also infer that the process would not remove dirt.

Q11.
Give a score of 0, 1, 2, or 3 based on how many plausible reasons are listed.
- Any reason that is based on information in the passage can be accepted.
- Possible answers could include that you have to comb the dog slowly, that there are many steps, that you comb the dog twice, that you brush the dog carefully, or that you have to condition the coat twice.

Q12.
Give a score of 0, 1, 2, or 3 based on how well the answer meets the criteria listed below.
- It should state whether the student would groom the dog themselves or pay a professional to do it.
- It should provide a fully-supported explanation of why the student made that decision.
- It should use relevant details from the passage.

PARCC Practice, Set 12, Short Literary Text

Question	Answer	Common Core Reading Standard for Literature
1	C	Determine the meaning of words and phrases as they are used in a text, including those that allude to significant characters found in mythology (e.g., Herculean).
2	B	Determine the meaning of words and phrases as they are used in a text, including those that allude to significant characters found in mythology (e.g., Herculean).
3	See Below	Refer to details and examples in a text when explaining what the text says explicitly and when drawing inferences from the text.
4	C	Refer to details and examples in a text when explaining what the text says explicitly and when drawing inferences from the text.
5	A	Determine the meaning of words and phrases as they are used in a text, including those that allude to significant characters found in mythology (e.g., Herculean).
6	C	Explain major differences between poems, drama, and prose, and refer to the structural elements of poems and drama when writing or speaking about a text.
7	A	Explain major differences between poems, drama, and prose, and refer to the structural elements of poems and drama when writing or speaking about a text.
8	C	Determine a theme of a story, drama, or poem from details in the text; summarize the text.
9	C	Refer to details and examples in a text when explaining what the text says explicitly and when drawing inferences from the text.
10	See Below	Refer to details and examples in a text when explaining what the text says explicitly and when drawing inferences from the text.
11	See Below	Make connections between the text of a story or drama and a visual or oral presentation of the text, identifying where each version reflects specific descriptions and directions in the text.
12	See Below	Determine a theme of a story, drama, or poem from details in the text; summarize the text.

Q3.
Give a score of 0, 1, or 2 based on how many correct lines are given. The correct lines are listed below.
- And turn your sadness into joy, / Make a smile from a frown. / And lifts you up when you are down. / To bring enjoyment out of sorrow,

Q10.
Give a score of 0, 1, or 2 based on how well the answer meets the criteria listed below.
- It should provide a clear and accurate explanation of what the statement means.
- The explanation should be related to how happiness can keep people feeling good during difficult times. The student should recognize that keeping warm is not meant literally.

Q11.
Give a score of 0, 1, or 2 based on how well the answer meets the criteria listed below.
- It should provide an analysis of how the photograph relates to the theme or the tone of the poem.
- The answer may refer to the image as helping to create a positive or uplifting tone, or may refer to the field of flowers as something simple and natural that suggests happiness.

Q12.
Give a score of 0, 1, 2, or 3 based on how well the answer meets the criteria listed below.
- It should summarize the main theme of the poem and explain what the poem teaches about happiness and sadness.
- It should include three reasons that it is important to keep smiling or to keep being happy. Possible reasons include that it can make you feel better during sad times, that you can share happiness with others, that it makes life more enjoyable, or that it helps you make the most of every day.
- It should use relevant details from the passage.

PARCC Practice, Set 13, Long Informational Text

Question	Answer	Common Core Reading Standard for Informational Text
1	B	Determine the meaning of general academic and domain-specific words or phrases in a text relevant to a grade 4 topic or subject area.
2	D	Refer to details and examples in a text when explaining what the text says explicitly and when drawing inferences from the text.
3	D	Compare and contrast a firsthand and secondhand account of the same event or topic; describe the differences in focus and the information provided.
4	C	Interpret information presented visually, orally, or quantitatively and explain how the information contributes to an understanding of the text in which it appears.
5	See Below	Refer to details and examples in a text when explaining what the text says explicitly and when drawing inferences from the text.
6	See Below	Determine the meaning of general academic and domain-specific words or phrases in a text relevant to a grade 4 topic or subject area.
7	B	Determine the main idea of a text and explain how it is supported by key details; summarize the text.
8	C	Determine the meaning of general academic and domain-specific words or phrases in a text relevant to a grade 4 topic or subject area.
9	See Below	Explain events, procedures, ideas, or concepts in a historical, scientific, or technical text, including what happened and why, based on specific information in the text.
10	See Below	Describe the overall structure (e.g., chronology, comparison, cause/effect, problem/solution) of events, ideas, concepts, or information in a text or part of a text.
11	See Below	Interpret information presented visually, orally, or quantitatively and explain how the information contributes to an understanding of the text in which it appears.
12	See Below	Explain how an author uses reasons and evidence to support particular points in a text.

Q5.
Give a score of 0.5 for each correct term circled. The correct terms are listed below.
- home plate, diamond, innings, strike zone

Q6.
Give a score of 0, 1, or 2 based on how many correct definitions are given.
- It should give a reasonable definition of any two of the correct terms for Question 5.

Q9.
Give a score of 0, 1, 2, or 3 based on how many correct roles are listed.
- Correct answers include whether players on the batting team are out, whether pitchers throw the ball correctly, whether pitchers have one foot on the pitcher's mound, and whether the ball passes through the strike zone.

Q10.
Give a score of 0, 1, or 2 based on how well the answer meets the criteria listed below.
- It should identify that the information in paragraph 5 describes the history of the game.
- It should compare this to the rest of the passage, which mainly teaches about the rules of baseball.

Q11.
Give a score of 0, 1, or 2 based on how well the answer meets the criteria listed below.
- It should provide an analysis of how the photograph helps show why an umpire is placed at each base.
- It should relate to how the photograph helps show that it could be difficult to determine whether the runner is safe.

Q12.
Give a score of 0, 1, 2, or 3 based on how well the answer meets the criteria listed below.
- It should state whether or not the student agrees that baseball is a great sport for young kids.
- It should include a fully-supported explanation of why the student agrees or disagrees.

PARCC Practice, Set 14, Paired Informational Passages

Question	Answer	Common Core Reading Standard for Informational Text
1	B	Determine the meaning of general academic and domain-specific words or phrases in a text relevant to a grade 4 topic or subject area.
2	B	Compare and contrast a firsthand and secondhand account of the same event or topic; describe the differences in focus and the information provided.
3	A	Determine the main idea of a text and explain how it is supported by key details; summarize the text.
4	See Below	Explain how an author uses reasons and evidence to support particular points in a text.
5	See Below	Determine the main idea of a text and explain how it is supported by key details; summarize the text.
6	See Below	Refer to details and examples in a text when explaining what the text says explicitly and when drawing inferences from the text.
7	C	Interpret information presented visually, orally, or quantitatively and explain how the information contributes to an understanding of the text in which it appears.
8	D	Determine the meaning of general academic and domain-specific words or phrases in a text relevant to a grade 4 topic or subject area.
9	B	Explain how an author uses reasons and evidence to support particular points in a text.
10	See Below	Describe the overall structure (e.g., chronology, comparison, cause/effect, problem/solution) of events, ideas, concepts, or information in a text or part of a text.
11	See Below	Refer to details and examples in a text when explaining what the text says explicitly and when drawing inferences from the text.
12	See Below	Integrate information from two texts on the same topic in order to write or speak about the subject knowledgeably.

Q4.
Give a score of 0, 1, or 2 based on how many correct details are given.
- The details may include that he composed over 600 pieces of music, that he wrote music for different instruments, that he wrote whole operas, that he produced concerts, that he became famous, or that he started composing music at age 5.

Q5.
Give a score of 0, 1, or 2 based on how many pairs of places and details are correctly listed.
- Paris   Searched for work / Wrote music
- Vienna   Wrote his best-known work / Wrote music, performed, and produced

Q6.
Give a score of 0, 1, or 2 based on how well the answer meets the criteria listed below.
- It should give a reasonable analysis of how Mozart's life can be considered sad.
- It may refer to how he was once unable to find work, how he managed his money poorly, how he spent his later years struggling, or how he died at the age of just 35.

Q10.
Give a score of 0, 1, or 2 based on how well the answer meets the criteria listed below.
- It should explain that the statue was too large and heavy to be placed on the roof of the Florence Cathedral.
- It should describe how the statue could not be lifted up to the roof, and may describe how machinery was not available at the time.

Q11.
Give a score of 0, 1, or 2 based on how well the answer meets the criteria listed below.
- It should make a reasonable inference about Michelangelo and his work based on how long it took him to complete the statue.
- The student may infer that Michelangelo was patient, careful, or wanted his work to be perfect. The student may also infer that his work was difficult.

Q12.
Give a score of 0, 1, 2, or 3 based on how well the answer meets the criteria listed below.
- It should describe at least one similarity between Mozart and Michelangelo, such as that they were both successful, both artists, or both created works that are still admired today.
- It should describe at least one difference between Mozart and Michelangelo, such as that they worked in different fields, were born in different times, or that Michelangelo was also talented in other areas.
- It should use relevant details from both passages.

CPSIA information can be obtained at www.ICGtesting.com
Printed in the USA
BVOW09s1738030416

442795BV00002B/8/P